art projects
for young children

By Jane A. Caballero, Ph.D

Elementary Education Department
University of Miami
Coral Gables, Florida

Art Director/Designer
Susan Fritts
Mechanical Artist
Trudy Miller

Humanics Limited
P.O. Box 7447
Atlanta, Georgia 30309

Library of Congress Card Catalog Number: 79-65813

PRINTED IN THE UNITED STATES OF AMERICA

ISBN 0-89334-051-0

Acknowledgements

My thanks go to Charles T. Caballero for his photography and and selected illustrations and to Dr. Emilio Caballero and Charles T. Caballero for their consultation in art education.

My thanks also go to my daughter, Lara, and to my students in the course Art for the Elementary School at the University of Miami for participation in the projects presented in this book.

Contents

CHAPTER 1 General Introduction

Art experiences play a vital role in the child's development, but do we really stop to think how much art affects the child's life?

Art builds perception. The child learns visual and tactile perception and artistic expression. Motor skills are developed— such as eye-hand coordination and large and small muscle development. We, as teachers, must not forget the basic purpose of art is to allow for self-expression. Other goals in our art program should include creativity, art history, visual and tactile perception, and developing a feeling for art (aesthetic judgment). For children, art is not only a form of expressing one's feelings but also a way of communicating ideas. Most children's art compositions relate to their experiences, how much they have observed, and what is important about a particular experience. A young child's work is not an objective representation but an emotional reaction to his environment. Therefore, the teacher can learn a great deal about children through their art. Their artistic development can be easily observed. The teacher may be able to recognize the different developmental levels of the child and thus be able to guide him, individually, toward maximum creative development. Lowenfeld, a noted art educator, has identified the stages of artistic development into the following categories. The scribbling stage is from approximately 2-4 years old. The child is only concerned with up and down motion. The color is unimportant. Soon he'll name the scribblings. To adults, the names might have no correlation to what is on the paper, but the child sees otherwise. The preschematic stage is from the approximate ages 4-6. Creation becomes conscious during this stage. The child controls his scribbles and begins naming them. He may exaggerate important parts in the drawing and use "unreal" color, size and proportion. The schematic stage is from the approximate ages 7-9. Representation with no intentional experiences is exhibited. More realism is apparent. The child discovers that he is part of the environment. The child draws through symbols. The next stage is the gang stage from the ages 9-11. The child finally becomes aware of reality and begins drawing what he sees[1].

Therefore, the teacher plays a vital role in the child's artistic development and expression. She should understand the stages of development and help children express themselves creatively. She should have an understanding of human growth and development so she can anticipate, understand and cope with the behavior of the child. She should know how to plan individual art activities and use better and clearer terminology.

The value of art activities for the young child lies primarily in the process of creation rather than in the finished product. This sense of accomplishment derived from successful manipulation of art media can help build self-confidence, a feeling of "I did this by myself. I enjoyed doing it. I'm pretty good." This is especially true if the child's creation is valued for itself and not compared to someone else's which might be more 'artistic' or representative, or to a model which an adult has in mind. Through experimentation and practice with some guidance, the child learns the possibilities, limits, and a beginning control of the media he uses. These learnings are important in themselves, and also as foundations for later learnings.

We must learn to respect children's art work. It has a distinct charm of its own. Children have a difficult time feigning the enjoyment of art, so we must be aware of a child who doesn't enjoy art and evaluate how we are presenting it. Remember children are not concerned with using color imitatively as it appears in nature and they do not draw things the way they look to adults. Therefore, there is no place for steretypes mimeographed outlines or coloring books. Every activity should be a creative experience which requires original thinking, planning, and doing. Children should be encouraged to create at their own speed and verbalize about what they are doing.

Remember all children have the potential for creative expression. It is the responsibility of parents and teachers to provide opportunities for this potential to develop as fully as possible. We must provide experiences in working with various drawing media (such as pastels, charcoal, crayons, and tempera paints) to encourage skill development as well as awareness of color. Children can work with fabrics and fibers learning simple tye-dye techniques, weaving and collages. Photography can be

[1]Lowenfeld, Viktor. *Creative and Mental Growth.* N.Y. The MacMillan Co., 1947.

used to emphasize sequencing and awareness of the surroundings. Cut and paste activities can encourage manipulative skill development and compositions. Children should help construct bulletin boards. This experience will provide them with knowledge about the subject of the board as well as compositional knowledge. Puppet-making can encourage creativity and help children learn to express themselves. Printing techniques such as finger prints, vegetables, sponge and cardboard prints, encourage children to discover thick and thin as well as learning the art of printmaking. Clay can allow for self-expression and success. It stirs the imagination and its resistance is challenging. Communication and sociability can be encouraged as children work together. The manipulation of the media encourages creativity. The following list of projects may be adapted to meet your student's needs.

Painting (tempera)
    color wheel, blends;
    projects: straw, blob, string, tissue paper

Painting (water color)
    washes, finger prints

Drawing (charcoal, pencil, India ink, pastels, crayons, felt pens) lines, expressive, contour, gesture, crayon resist, still-life, body completion, face, perspective

Clay (modeling, ceramics)
    pinch, coil, slab techniques, wedging, firing, glazing processes

Printing (finger, leaf, cardboard, linoleum, vegetable)
    vacabulary, techniques

Cut and Paste (shapes, expanding, fastening, cutouts, symmetrical, sculture)
    murals, mosaic, flowers, papér-maché, miscellaneous projects

Puppets (stick, sack, papér-maché, plate sock, fold paper, plate, sock, fold paper, hand puppet)
    language objectives, history, puppet stages

Photography (media experience with visuals and equipment)
    family tree, slides, color blend, flip book,

frame/mount, opaque/transparent

Visual file (utilizing magazines, personal photographs)
classification of pictures, collages

Fabric/fiber (batik, tye-dye)
yarn, material collage, weaving

Bulletin boards (guidelines, suggestions, flannel boards)
seasonal, subjects, rules, people, 3-D boxes

Lettering techniques
cutting, forming, writing

Art appreciation (the child should be familiar with an overview of artists, art periods, and special topics which
can enhance his awareness of this aspect of art.)

Evaluation of the art program must be carefully
considered. Considerations should include:

• The quality of each pupil's personal artistic expression
• The quality of each pupil's reaction to the work of others
• The quality of each pupil's behavior as exhibited during
his/her participation in all types of art activities.

The teacher should realize that he will most likely be
wrong in his appraisal of the child's patterns of behavior and
his ability to produce and appreciate art. The most effective
way of developing as a teacher of art is growth through
teaching practice. Efficiency of art teaching and the teacher's
professional growth go hand in hand. Learning to understand
children is made easier through the arts. It provides an
excellent means for observing the behavior of children.
Because the free creative expressions of children are
projections of their personalities, art products offer revealing
insights into the more complex factors of the children's
organizations. Sometimes we need to examine how we feel
about what we saw, or how someone we're trying to draw
might feel.

We must remember that the central purpose of the art
program is to provide children with a vehicle to wholesome
personality development and enriched living. But the deepest
educational insight will be achieved only when the subject
matter and the technique are developed from the most direct
experiences possible.

EVALUATION CHART/Scribbling Stage

Ages 2-4 Years

INTELLECTUAL GROWTH

Are there uncontrolled lines only?
Does he only pound or knead clay?

Are all motions controled, repeated motions: longitudinal or circular?
Does he form coils with clay?
Does he enjoy breaking the clay?

Does the child name his scribbling?
Does he name his pieces of clay?

EMOTIONAL GROWTH

Does the child enjoy his scribbling?
Is the scribbling free from stereotyped repetitions?
Is the scribbling free from interrupted lines?
Are the child's motions determined and forceful?
Does the intensity and direction of the motions change?

SOCIAL GROWTH

Does the child concentrate on his motions?
Is it difficult to divert the child?

PERCEPTUAL GROWTH

Does the child show the desire for large motions? (Kinesthetic freedom)
Does the child enjoy tactile sensations when working with clay?
Does the child control his motions visually?
When he names his scribbling, does he use different colors to differ-
entiate different meanings?

PHYSICAL GROWTH

Are the motions vigorous?
Are the lines bold?
Does the child use his whole arm?

AESTHETIC GROWTH

Does the child distribute his motions over the whole paper?

Does the child show a feeling for balance in his distribution of dense and loose scribbling?

CREATIVE GROWTH

Is the child independent in his scribbling?

When scribbling with other children, does the child remain uninfluenced?

Is he generally opposed to imitating?

When naming his scribbling, does he develop stories independently?

EVALUATION CHART/Pre-Schematic Stage

Ages 4-7 Years

INTELLECTUAL GROWTH

Does the child's representation of a man show more than head and feet?
Does the child draw more than head, body, arms, legs, features?

Are eyes, nose, mouth indicated?
Are the features represented with different representative symbols?
As compared with the previous drawings is there an increase of details?
(Active Knowledge.)
Is the child's drawing representational?
Does the drawing show details?

EMOTIONAL GROWTH

Does the child frequently change his concepts for "man," "tree," or details like "eye," "nose," etc?
Does the Child form stereotyped repetitions?
Are parts which are important to the child somewhat exaggerated?
Is there a lack of continuity and too much exaggeration?
Is the drawing definite in lines and color, showing the child's confidence in his work?
Does the child relate things which are important to him?

SOCIAL GROWTH

Is the child's work related to a definite experience?
Is there any order determined by emotional relationships?
Does the child show spatial correlations: sky above, ground below?
Does the child show awareness of a particular environment (home, school, etc.)?

PERCEPTUAL GROWTH

Does the child use lines other than geometric? (Lines when separated from the whole do not lose meaning.)
Does the child indicate movements or sounds?
Does the child relate color to objects?
Does the child start in his modeling from the whole lump of clay?

PHYSICAL GROWTH

Is there continuous omission of the same body part?
Is there continuous exaggeration of the same body part?
Are the child's lines determined and vigorous?
Does the child include body actions?

AESTHETIC GROWTH

Is the meaningful space well distributed against the meaningless space?
Does the organization of the subject matter seem equally important to its content?
Do colors appear to be distributed decoratively?
Does the child show a desire for decoration?

CREATIVE GROWTH

Does the child use his independent concepts?
If the child works in a group, does he remain uninfluenced?
When the child is alone does he spontaneously create in any medium?
When the child is alone does he refrain from imitating for imitation's sake?

EVALUATION CHART/Schematic Stage

Ages 7-9 Years

INTELLECTUAL GROWTH

Has the child developed concepts for things familar to him?
Are his concepts clearly expressed?
Has he a tendency to differentiate his schemata? (Hands with fingers, eyes with eyebrows, etc.)
Does the child relate colors to objects?

EMOTIONAL GROWTH

Does the child use his schemata flexibly?
Does the child vary the sizes according to the significance of the represented objects?
Does the drawing show deviations from the schema by exaggerating, omitting, or even changing meaningful parts?
Does the child use his lines or brush strokes in a determined fashion?
Is there a lack of continuous "folding over?"
Is there a lack of continued over-exaggeration?

SOCIAL GROWTH

Does he identify himself with his own experience?
Has the child established spatial correlations?
Does the child use base lines?
Does the child characterize his environment?
Does the child show awareness of his social environment in identifying himself with others?

PERCEPTUAL GROWTH

Does the child mostly draw with continued uninterrupted lines, expressing kinesthetic sensations?
Is the child aware of differences in texture?
Does the child depart from the use of mere geometric lines?
Does the child show visual awareness by drawing distant objects smaller?
Does the child differentiate his color-object relationships? (Does he use different greens for different plants and trees?)
Does the child model analytically?

PHYSICAL GROWTH

Does the child show body actions in his drawings?
Does the child show the absence of continuous exaggerations of the same body parts?

Does the child show other signs which indicate his sensitivity toward the use of his body? (Joints, special details.)
Does the child guide his brush strokes so that he remains within the predetermined area?

AESTHETIC GROWTH

Does the child unconsciously utilize his drive for repetition for design purposes?
Does the child distribute his work over the whole sheet?
Does the child think in terms of the whole drawing when he draws—not in terms of single details only?
Does the child use decorative patterns?

CREATIVE GROWTH

Does the child create his own representative symbols (concepts)?
Does the child vary his schemata?
Does the child frequently change his symbols for eyes, nose, mouth, etc.?
Does the child invent his own topics? (Lowenfeld, 1947)

Scribbling Stage

Pre-Schematic Stage

Schematic Stage

Categories of Criteria Used in Appraisal of the Art Program

1. The quality of each pupil's personal artistic expression.
    A. To what extent has the pupil attempted to express his reactions to his own experiences?
    B. To what extent has he expressed himself emotionally and intellectually?
    C. To what extent has the pupil developed a personal style or technique?
    D. To what extent does the pupil's work show a sensitivity concerning functional design?

2. The quality of each pupil's reaction to the work of others.
    A. To what extent does the pupil look at the work of his classmates and of professionals, and what appears to be his attitude toward his own work?
    B. To what extent does he consult books of art?
    C. What is his apparent attitude toward art, as shown in his reaction to films, slides, talks, and visits to institutions?
    D. What evidence of a satisfactory development of taste has he shown?

3. The quality of each pupil's behavior as exhibited during his participation in all types of art activities.
    A. During his art activities, in what respect has the pupil demonstrated a personal initiative?
    B. To what extent does he find a challenge in unfamiliar art materials?
    C. In what respects has he demonstrated through art activities, an inner discipline, worthy habits of thinking, commendable attitudes regarding a search for excellence, or other desirable personal qualities?
    D. To what extent does he show good judgment in selecting tools and media for art work?
    E. Once having selected an artistic goal, to what extent does he strive to reach it?
    F. To what extent has he demonstrated qualities of leadership in art activities?
    G. What is his attitude with regard to accepting advice about his artistic production?
    H. To what extent has he shown himself willing to cooperate generally in the worthly art projects of his group?

I. How willing is he to share in research work in art, in expressive work, and in less rewarding tasks such as helping to keep equipment, supplies, and the work area used by the group clean and tidy? In general, does he seem willing to share ideas about art with others?

J. Has he shown a reasonable attitude toward the sharing of display space?

The Teacher of Art

New programs, classrooms and equipment are signs of progress, but the individual teacher is still the most vital factor in all our learning experiences. She should be the inspired one, creating and adapting new techniques, lighting the flame for greater achievement. This book tries to present practical suggestions within the basic principles of free expression for young students of art.

Creative art activities are based on the same precepts that apply to other forms of education. The teacher and group leaders have an even greater opportunity for devising new techniques in developing the creative instincts of students.

The following projects allow a great deal of freedom and expression of self, therefore allowing much enjoyment for children. They require no special skill and will hold the interest of children.

CHAPTER 2
Drawing

A line is a mark made by a moving point. Some materials that that you can experiment with may include: white drawing paper, oak tag, construction paper, felt tip pens, pen and ink,conte crayon, pencil, chalk, crayon, charcoal, yarn and string.

Sample activities may include:

1. Drawing lines: expressive–play a musical selection and draw any desired subject; texture–close, detailed lines; directional lines–draw 1, 2, or 3 directions to show variety and textures; contour–one countinuous line that creates a boundary between a space and its background.

2. Cutting out part of a human body from a magazine (one half of the figure may be desirable). Glue it on paper and let the child draw the rest of the person. Body awareness is emphasized.

3. Looking at an object, person, or still life. You may want to draw the face of the person or do a gesture showing the action or movement.

4. One and two-point perspective drawings may be introduced.

5. Experimenting with crayon resist. Color on a paper with random color; press hard. Paint on top with black tempera, India ink or black crayon. Scratch through with a pointed object. A paper clip may be used if young children are doing the activity.

6. Drawing a picture with glue and place yarn or string on top.

Contour drawing is for older students. It is done by having the student look at an object and draw it without looking at the paper. Contour drawing emphasises control. It strengthens the child's ability to really "see" something. Many details are omitted in contour drawings because the emphasis is on the shape or contour of the object.

The drawing below was done with India ink and brush. The purpose is to expose the child to different materials that can be used to draw with. Ink and brush lines cary in thickness and produce a tectural effect.

These two examples are of gesture drawing. The child simply looks at the person to be drawn and quickly draws the body with circular motions relative to the muscular positions. The drawing should be done in a matter of seconds. The purpose is to acquaint the child with body movements and linear representation of them.

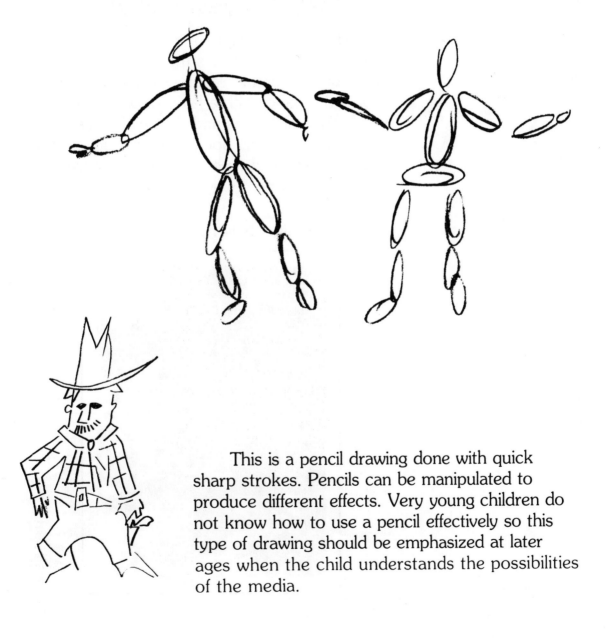

This is a pencil drawing done with quick sharp strokes. Pencils can be manipulated to produce different effects. Very young children do not know how to use a pencil effectively so this type of drawing should be emphasized at later ages when the child understands the possibilities of the media.

This is an example of a crayon resist drawing. The child colors the entire piece of paper with different crayon colors and then covers the paper with a layer of black tempera paint. The paint dries and the child can scratch in a design with any pointed instrument. Young children enjoy this type of activity because it is a completely different way of drawing.

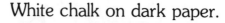

White chalk on dark paper.

Precise and definite paint and brush lines.
Warm colors advance, cool colors recede. Lines
reflect movement of the work. Crayons vary
thickness and color in lines.

Experimenting with
various media. India ink
and tempera paint; cray-
ons; pastels. (Pastels may
be placed in a 1 to 3 part
sugar water solution to
prevent the pastels from
smearing and rubbing
off.)

Soft, blurred chalk lines.

This is an example of a child's pencil and crayon drawing. It shows the child's family and home as he interprets them. The child was in the schematic stage of art development.

The child may draw with Elmer's glue then place yarn or string onto the outline.

Cut out part of the human body from a magazine. Glue it on the paper. The child may draw the rest of the figure. Body awareness is emphasized. (It may be desirable to cut the figure vertically down the midline; and let the child complete the figure if he has difficulty; with the body parts.)

Two point perspective example. Perspective may be introduced to children on the upper-elementary level. Their artistic level of development will prevent them from understanding prior to this time.

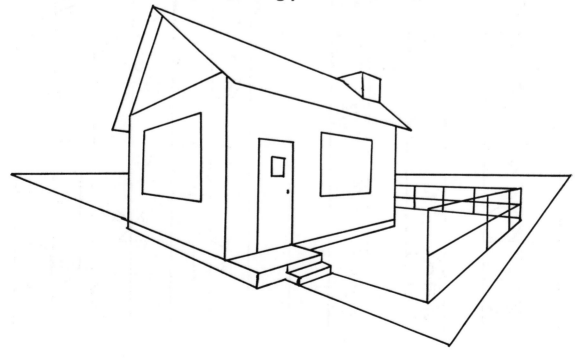

An excellent exercise in drawing is to practice the basic manuscript strokes.

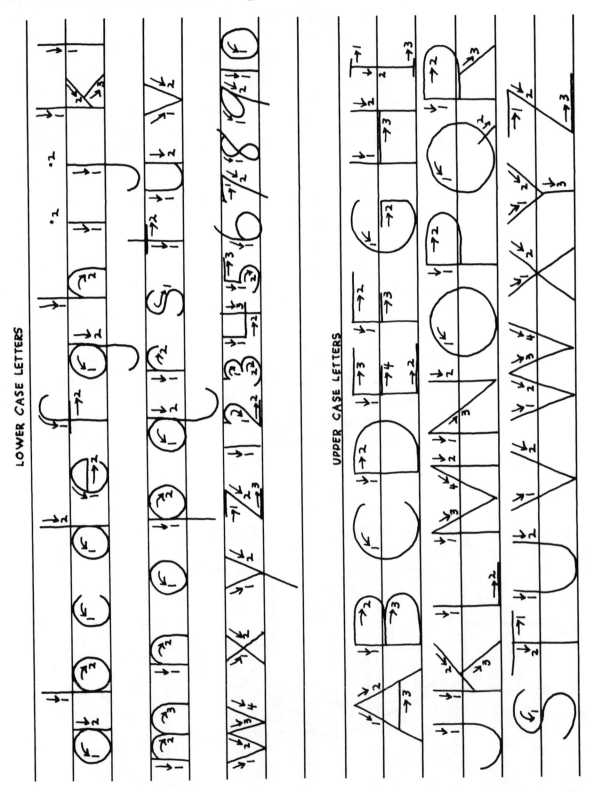

MAKING SMOCKS FOR ART:

To make smocks for children to use in art, go to upholstery shops and ask them to save scraps of vinyl for you.

You can cut these as illustrated:

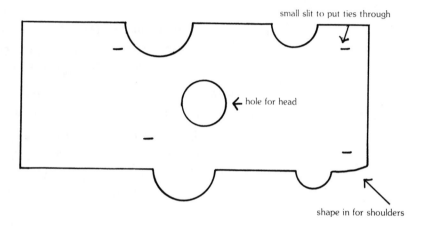

Ties may be about 2 in. wide and about 8 in. long.

The poncho style could also be used.

These vinyl smocks are easy to wipe clean and last for years.

CHAPTER 3 Painting

COLOR WHEEL

The child learns the concept of primary, secondary and intermediate colors through the creation of the color wheel. Making a color wheel lets the child experiment with color combinations, and demonstrates the formation of specific colors through mixing. Vocabulary words including hue, primary color, secondary and intermediate colors, neutral, blend, intensity, warm and cool colors can be introduced to the students.

COLOR KEY

○ Primary
□ Secondary
△ Intermediate

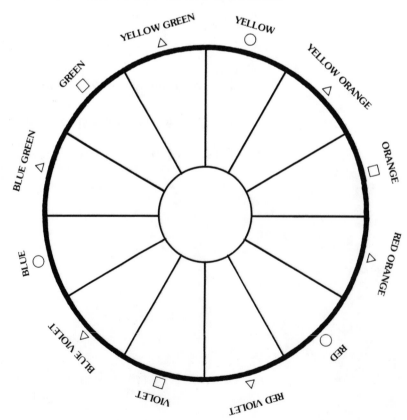

VALUE CHANGE

Using the concept of value change demonstrates for the child the idea of darkest and lightest values of a hue. By mixing white and black neutrals with a given hue the child becomes aware of the many possible shades of a given color.

NEUTRAL BLEND

A neutral blend shows the value scale of black and white. Its concepts are the same as those of the value change scale except that two neutrals are mixed.

INTENSITY CHANGE

Through the mixing of a primary and a secondary color, the child becomes aware of the different intensities of color. The child can then see that the two complementary colors can be mixed to produce shades of varying intensities and can also arrive at a neutral shade.

WARM AND COOL BLENDS

Mixing the warm and cool colors produce for the child an example of blends. The child learns to associate the warm colors together and the cool colors together. The child also becomes aware of the applications of these blends to emphasize certain qualities in paintings.

BLOB PAINTING

This easy painting emphasizes for the child the idea of symmetrical balance. It also may show the blending of colors to form various hues when more than one color is used. The unusual shapes created by blob painting are pleasing and interesting to the child.

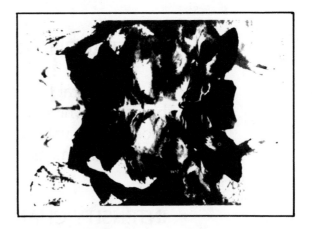

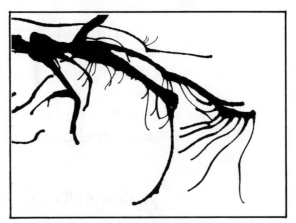

STRAW BLOWING PAINTING

This teaches the child control of his fine muscles as he manipulates the straw. An interesting design is created and thickness and thinness of line is emphasized.

SUGAR AND CHALK PAINTING

Materials needed: sugar
                   chalk (colored)
                   water

Procedure: Dissolve one part sugar in three parts water and place in pans for soaking the chalk. Soak chalk for a few minutes then remove from water.

Once the chalk is soaked it can be used instead of paint. The advantages of this is that the children will be able to draw an object easier, and quickly fill in all the areas. It dries quickly on paper, and the colors do not tend to run into each other and smear. If the chalk becomes dry while the children are using them, they may be dipped in the sugar-and-water solution and be reactivated. The finished pictures do not rub off as regular chalk drawings do.

SUGAR AND CHALK PAINTING

This method of painting is useful when the regular painting materials are not available. This method may be easier for some children because they can control the medium more effectively.

WATERCOLOR

Supplies Needed

Watercolor paper: Cold press is best for texture, 140 lb. (student grade) 300 lb. is better but expensive.

Brushes: 1" soft flat; 2" soft flat; 1/4" soft flat; #10 and #8 round sable; Sable Script Liner.

Paint: Box or tube watercolors (Grumbacher Finest tube paints are best because they mix true).

Water container: One large enough to dip sponge into; remember to keep water clean.

Sponge, kleenex, napkins, rags, masking tape or brown paper tape, pallette, drawing board (large enough for your paper!)

Washes:

Standard flat wash

   a. all same value
   b. not much variety in texture
   c. mix up enough wash in cup before starting
   d. Start at top of sheet with brush fully loaded and make stroke after stroke

Graded wash

   a. goes from light to dark or dark to light
   b. start with dark pigment and water on dry paper
   c. add more water (clean water) after each stroke

Vocabulary

WASH A mixture of water and paint, of light value, and laid on first to block in an area.

OVER-LAY After one color dries, apply another color wash on over it.

MUDDY	A murky mixture of colors due to the application of too many color washes put over each other (never use more than 3 colors laid over each other).
HARD EDGE	Stopping a wash too quickly and not blending the color out with water before it dries.
BLOSSOM	Dropping water or paint into a wet area causing it to run or blorssom—to form an area with fuzzy edges.
WET ON WET	Keeping the paper wet at all times so that the color will bleed into another forming soft lines.
BLEEDING	Letting one color run freely into another.
WET AND DRY	Letting the paper dry before adding detail on wet over-lays.
BLOT	Using a towel, napkins, or tissues to lighten wet colors, to remove wet colors, or to stop bleeding. Helps bring out highlights.
FOREGROUND	Area of the painting closest to you.
MIDDLE-GROUND	The area in the middle of the painting.
BACKGROUND	Area in the painting furthest away from you.

WATERCOLOR WASH:

This technique involves using small amounts of watercolor with large doses of water. The colors are simply "washed" across the sheet of paper. In this example, India ink was applied after the wash dried and the lines were used to create a picture.

This technique is similar to a wash. A wet flat brush is used to lay in the trunk of the tree, Half of the brush is dipped in a light color and the other half is dipped in a dark color. When the brush is stroked onto the wet trunk, the colors blend. A script liner may be used to extend branches using the wet pigment on the trunk.

This picture shows another watercolor technique or painting. It involves the use of tissues and watercolors. The paper is wet and then the tissue is applied to form mountain shapes. Watercolor is then added to define the outline and texture of the mountains by bleeding through the tissue. The rest of the picture is watercolor wash of wet on wet. Trees and houses may be added if desired.

Straw Blowing Painting with finger prints.

Finger prints using watercolors. Leaf prints and India ink add
to the composition.

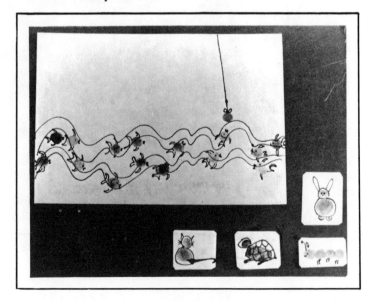

TISSUE PAPER PAINTING

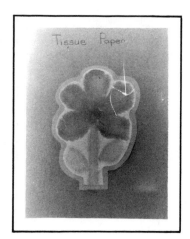

This is yet another method of painting when regular materials are not accessible. The child simply arranges tissue paper pieces on a paper and then applies small amounts of water to soak the pieces, then the tissue paper is lifted off and the coloration remains as a finished product. As in regular painting, colors can be mixed by overlapping and colors may run together to create an interesting effect.

CHAPTER 4
Cut and Paste

Paper is a wonderfully inspiring material, challenging to the imagination, vital as a medium for man's expressive purposes, yet essential for serving a vast amount of the world's utilitarian needs. Its importance as a vehicle for communication is evident, since it is a basic medium for transmitting news and information, thoughts and ideas, through letters, circulars, books, periodicals, and newspapers.

In many communities of the world, paper has become essential in the cultural pattern and a source of artistic enrichment within local traditions. The paper cutouts of Poland, for instance, renowned for their vitality and expressiveness, have long been recognized as a folk art.

Paper art has flourished in many countries. The making of silhouettes, for example, was once an art sponsored in convents throughout Europe. Painters have found paper useful for cutting shapes to be studied and related as they plan the composition of their pictures.

The creation of art is the creation of true vitality, and the controlling factor in arriving at standards of judgment is design. A constantly growing sensitivity to everything we come into contact with is necessary in order to encourage good design and improve standards of taste.

Education should provide opportunities for the creative impulses of all to find expression through suitable materials.

PAPER SCULPTURE

When paper came into common use, it was employed for many forms of decoration. With the coming of machinery, paper was further enbellished for use as lace, finely etched valentines, and as holders for formal Victorian posies. In all these forms of art with the exception of the paper frills and the nineteenth century "paper plastics," paper was used flat. More recently artists have used it three-dimensionally for interior decorations and for publicity purposes. For use in teaching children paper sculpture, the most important fact to keep in mind is that paper has unlimited richness of expression, but a limited range of form. Realism must be excluded and every subject taken from nature translated into the unique language of paper.

Paper usually doesn't do exactly what you want it to unless forms are used that can be translated in this medium. The chosen subject should be chosen with care – don't choose the impossible! Paper gives a representation – not an imitation, therefore, working with paper is entirely different from techniques used when working with plaster, wood or metal.

Paper bends easily but always in one direction and always in a more or less geometrical form. The edges can be curved to a certain extent because the sides sloping down from them automatically follow the line. If handled otherwise the paper is liable to tear or crumble.

Children can be creative and original in making three-dimensional objects from cut paper if given only a few simple directions. Scissors, good quality paper, (which is smooth and pliable), paper punch, stapler pins and paper fasteners, glue and tape are all that is needed to give children a satisfying method of expression.

CUTTING A SQUARE

Bring side **A** of a rectangle to side **BC** and cut off extra piece below.

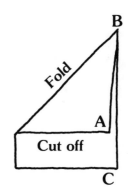

CUTTING A CIRCLE

Fold a square in half on the diagonal, forming a triangle. Fold in half again, and then in half again. Using **AB** as a measure, mark ac, ad and ae and cut a connecting arc.

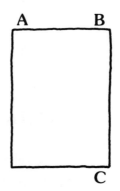

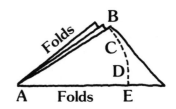

CUTTING A TRIANGLE

For an equilateral triangle, fold a rectangle in the center to get line ab. Draw a line **CE** the same length as cd and connect points **ED**. Or take the radius of a circle, **AB**, and mark off six times around the circumference Connect every other point.

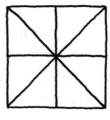

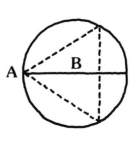

I feel that this is the basic beginning of paper work in art. This particular section is good in that it helps to build basic concepts of such things as fold, square, circle and triangle. A child should learn to do these basic things first.

SYMMETRICAL CUTTING

A child might be interested in doing this type of thing, in that he could use his imagination and cut his own designs.

Some structures are pure in form, while others are impressions derived from nature, like the butterfly shape used here for a subject source.

C

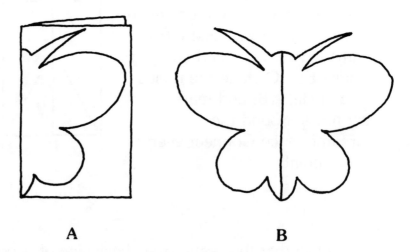

A   B

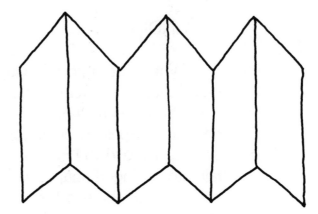

For the multiple-fold cut, the paper is folded a number of times and cut, with enough of the fold retained to enforce the structure. This is a good way of working rhythm into art.

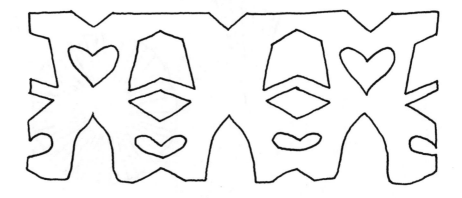

EXPANDING

When cut in certain ways, paper can be stretched and expanded into new and different shapes. A circle folded and cut toward the center will fall into a fringed shape, varied according to the width of the strips and the weight of paper used. A shape cut by following the contour from the outside edge toward the center will automatically be extended into a long form (diagrams B&C). For the plan in diagram D, a square or rectangle is folded and cut alternately from opposite end along the fold edge. In diagrams E, F and G, a square, a rectangle, and a circle are shown, folded several times and cut on alternate lines from opposite edges.

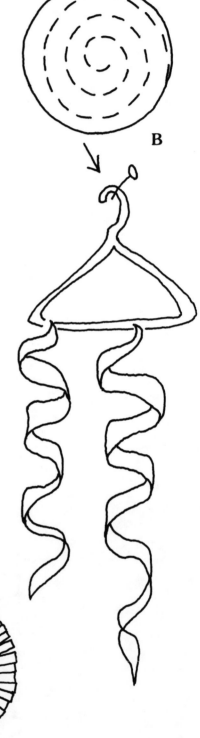

B

A

This assignment will not be too complicated, therefore, the child should not become frustrated. The child can do all of this work himself.

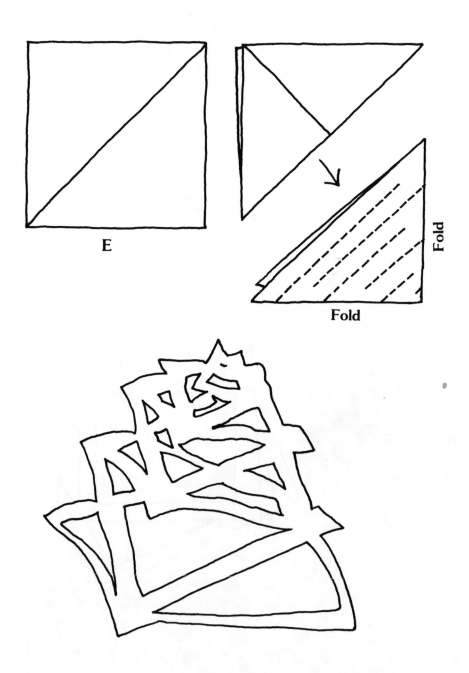

E

Fold

Fold

F

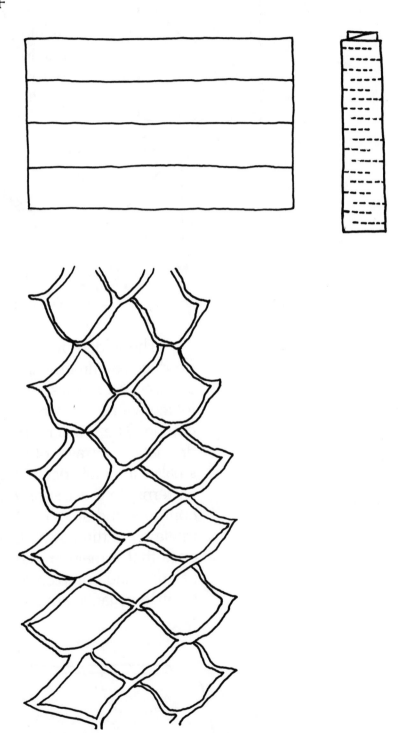

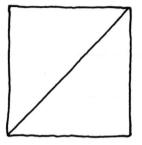

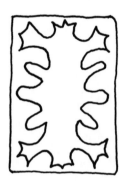

Cutouts are fascinating and would hold the interest of must children. This project is simple, but not so simple as to be an insult to a child's intelligence.

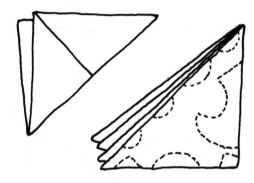

The folded paper technique, which always produces symmetrical shapes, is shown in squares, rectangles, and circles that have been folded alternately lengthwise and across for cutting. The resulting cutout openings make for dramatic contrasts of values, with larger and smaller intervals occurring in the rhythmic patterns. Interest is produced through varying the contours and sizes of shapes. The dark areas made by cutting away the paper and the light ones that remain are equal in interest and balance and complement each other, creating positive-negative shape relationships.

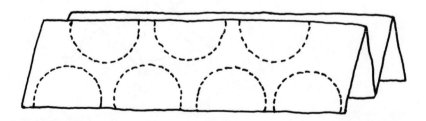

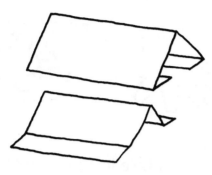

Paste tabs down.

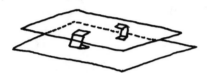

Paste tabs be-
tween sheets to
hold them apart.

WAYS TO FASTEN THINGS TOGETHER

There are a number of ways of attaching one piece of paper to another. Brads, pins, paper clips, needle and thread, and staples are among the mechanical means available. Tiny staples are helpful for reaching into unusually small openings, while long staplers are advisable for more extensive spaces. Sometimes it is more convenient to use pieces of tape, especially in inaccessible places where a stapler will not reach. Tape is handy for temporary purposes or for expediency. Paper can be fastened by tabs shown on this page, and slits, illustrated on the following page.

Bend paper to form tabs

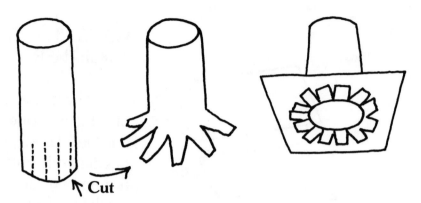

Push cylinder through hole in paper, and paste tabs.

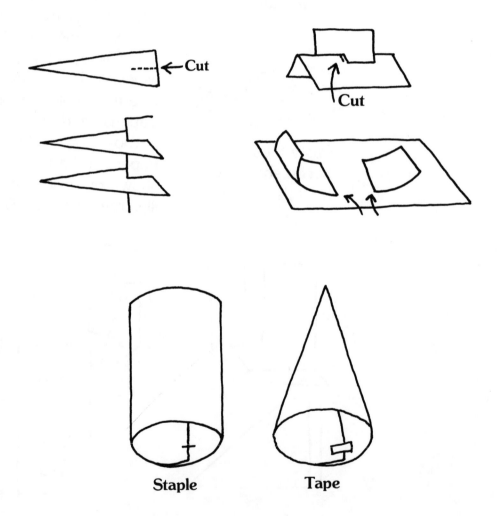

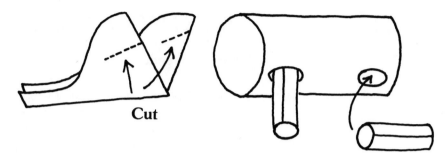

Cut

Cut slits on dotted lines and slip onto edge of big cylinder. Insert cylinders into holes.

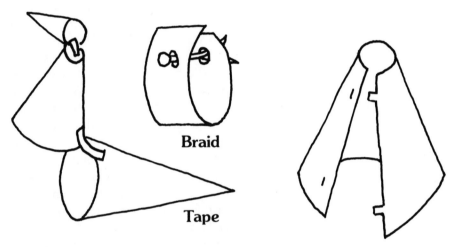

Braid

Tape

Insert tabs into slits. Use paste to hold.

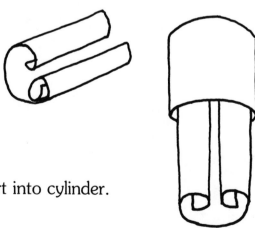

Roll paper and insert into cylinder.

PAPIER-MACHE ANIMALS

Materials Needed:

Wheat paste (consistency of whipping cream) in pans; newspapers; paper towels; masking tape; tempera paint; shellac decorations.

Tear newspaper and towels into strips 1" x 6". With dry newspaper make a ball the size of the animal's body. Cover this with a thick coat of wheat paste. Completely cover with two layers of paper strips that have been dipped in wheat paste. Roll and tape two pieces and newspaper thick enough and long enough to go over body and hang below for animal's legs. Flatten the two rolls as they cross the body and allow the four legs to stay round. Use paste and more wet stripes.

Fasten the legs in place. Make a smaller ball of paper for the head and attach it to the body with strips of paper that have been dipped in the wheat paste. It may be best to put the animal aside to dry overnight as this time as the maché is quite soft. Mold ears, tail, and any other features from small pieces of paper towel dipped in wheat paste. Add each to the dry animal, then cover the entire animal with wheat paste, adding strips of the absorbent towel until they have entirely covered the animal and are wet with the wheat paste. Add more paste if necessary. Smooth the surface, and apply paint when animal is thoroughly dry.

Other decorations can be added for variety and interest. Dots of color construction paper, shapes made of tissue paper, yarns, buttons, etc. can be used before painting the animal with shellac. Children have great imagination in decorating these animals and are delighted when they are used in a zoo or circus display.

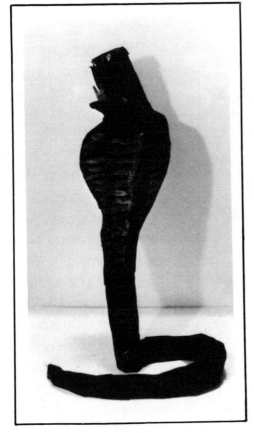

Puppet heads can be made by putting a few layers of the torn newspaper over a blown up balloon. Allow to dry; pop the balloon, and decorate. A circular piece of material attached at the base will complete the puppet.

NOTE: Remember to leave a small opening at the bottom of the bottom of the balloon for your fingers.

Murals can be used in the classroom for bulletin boards. Each student makes his own part, and the class puts it together on the bulletin board or a long sheet of butcher paper.

These pieces are from the mural based on the album, *The Point* by Nilsson. The album was played, then the children used their imagination to illustrate the sequence of this story.

Nilsson, Harry. *The Point*; Dunbar Music, Inc., 1970.

Bulletin board using the expanding paper concept.

Tissue paper picture. Overlapping creates new colors.

The star is created by laying string into the star shape on a piece of wax paper. Then glue with food coloring is painted onto the surface. The glue may be diluted. When it dries a transparent effect is achieved.

The light switch is made from strips of paper and yarn glued on the switch and painted. antiquing and shellac may be added for a final touch. This method looks nice over bottles, boxes, or other objects.

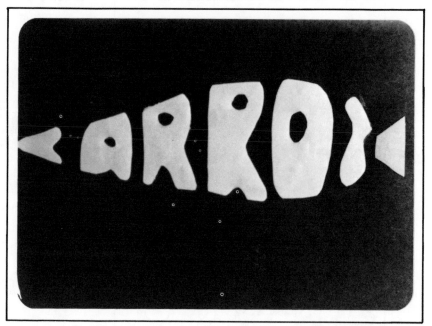

Cutting letters in the shape of a figure.

Mosaics-good clean-up activity after other cut and paste activity. Small scraps may be stored in boxes at the art center.

Gum wrapper chains (construction paper)
help develop coordination and shape awareness.

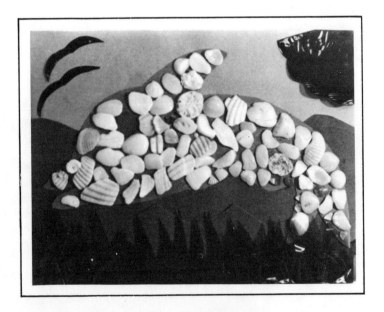

Collage may be made with any found objects
in addition to paper and glue. Clear or colored
cellophane paper adds interest.

Paper dolls, paper hats, paper mats and putting chains together all provide the child with basic skills of coordination, shapes, left-right progression and color.

MAKING PAPER FLOWERS

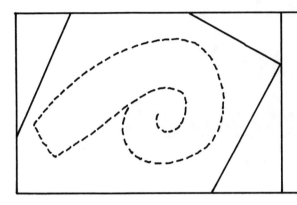

Using colorful medium
weight paper, draw free-
hand a curved figure similar
to above one.

Cut out along dotted line.
Take a ruler and curl with
edge as pictured.

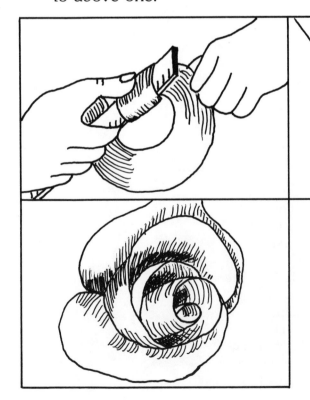

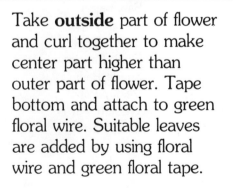

Take **outside** part of flower
and curl together to make
center part higher than
outer part of flower. Tape
bottom and attach to green
floral wire. Suitable leaves
are added by using floral
wire and green floral tape.

CHAPTER 5
Flannel and Bulletin Boards

Flannel Boards

It has been said that the child remembers FIVE times as much of what he sees than of what he hears only.

Types of Flannel Boards

Wall boards
Easel boards
Desk boards
Individual boards

Self-Adhering Materials

Blotters
Sandpaper
Rough Paper
Emery Paper
Flock Paper
Suede Paper
Velour Paper
Woolen Yarns
Rough String
Pipe Cleaners
Rough Rope
Felt

Corduroy
Chore Girl
Cotton
Burlap
Monks Cloth
Blanket Materials
Velvet
Balsa Wood
Steel Wool
Light Sponge
Cellophane
Suede Cloth

What are some of the advantages of the Flannel Board?

Easy to make
Inexpensive to buy
Can be arranged, rearranged, and stored easily
Adaptable to all ages
Permits child participation
Permits action
Can be manipulated by anyone
Attracts attention
Stimulates interest
Flexible in use
Easy to use
Improves communication – "A picture is worth a thousand words."

The degree of effectiveness is related directly to the skill and imagination of the teacher who decides what must be taught and how the material can best be communicated.

GUIDELINES FOR BULLETIN BOARDS

1. Use the bulletin board as a "point clincher."
2. Change the display frequently.
3. Keep material up-to-date.
4. Change the subject area often.
5. Start with an idea rather than material.
6. Build the display around a central theme or idea.
7. Use seasonal and holiday themes when practical.
8. Secure assistance from consultants, other teachers, and students.
9. Secure display ideas from advertisers, current periodicals, and professional magazines.
10. Plan the display carefully before placing it on the board.
11. Avoid the use of excessive printed materials.
12. Use brief, thought provoking captions.
13. Make use of unusual materials for captions.
14. Try the use of a question as your caption to attract attention.
15. Involve the readers, if possible, in the caption to attract attention.
16. Inject humor occasionally.
17. Make the arrangement attractive.

18. Avoid crowding the display.
19. Use blank space for emphasis.
20. Observe margin rules in arranging the display.
21. Make labels brief and effective.
22. Keep the display neat in appearance.
23. Hide the mechanics (pins, staples, etc.) on the display.
24. Attach bulletin board materials securely.
25. Use a variety of materials to create and maintain interest.
26. Make frequent use of 3-D materials.
27. Use attractive color combinations.
28. Maintain color harmony throughout the display.
29. Mount pictures and objects for attractiveness and preservation.
30. Encourage student participation.
31. Organize and use student committees (upper grades) in making bulletin board displays.
32. Keep a file of good bulletin board materials in order that they may be used again on appropriate occasions.
33. Develop an awareness of and desire for new materials.
34. Collect and file usable display materials for future use.

MAKE THE BULLETIN BOARD YOUR ASSISTANT!

BULLETIN BOARD SUGGESTIONS

CAPTIONS

Captions should attract attention, hold interest, and impress favorably.

Interesting captions . . .

1. Are brief and free from unnecessary words;
2. Invole the viewer in a question or problem;
3. Use unusual word combinations and clever phrases;
4. Contrast with background, light against dark, dark against light.

Unusual and interesting captions can be made from a variety of materials.

1. Letters can be cut from . . .

Construction paper
Corrugated paper
Wall paper
Newspaper
Finger painted paper
Spatter painted paper
Cardboard
Road maps
Magazine illustrations
Foil

Felt
Fabric (Glue to cardboard
     before cutting)
Cork
Styrofoam
Linoleum
Sponge
Sandpaper
Carpeting

2. Letters can be formed from . . .

Copper wire
Pipe cleaners
Twigs
Colored toothpicks
Ribbon
Clothes line

Rope
Raffia
Beverage straws
String
Twisted crepe paper

Macaroni (Soaked in cold water a few minutes before forming letters)
Carpet warp (Dipper in starch and then forming letters on wax paper)
Yarn (Write words with glue and then place yarn on glue)

3. Letters can be made with . . .

Felt pen
Prepared cut-out letters (Gummed back)
Wricco plastic stencils
      Signmaker (Large size lettering)
      Wricoprint (Small size lettering)
Dry transfer letters
Cardboard stencils
Stencils and spray painting

SUGGESTIONS FOR CREATING THE 3-D EFFECT

Many bulletin boards are designed entirely around flat materials (photos, illustrations, drawings, paper charts).

In order to avoid surface monotony, some of the flat material being displayed should be raised from the face of the bulletin board. There are numerous ways to accomplish this:

Scored tagboard

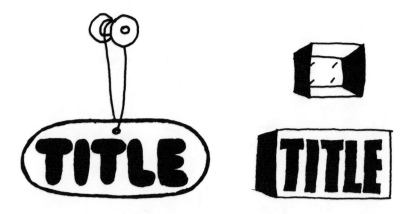

Attach a spool to the bulletin board and hang the title from the spool with yarn or string.

Staple free form with title on it to box; staple box to board, then place lid on the box.

Fasten the title to a piece of wire and staple the wire to the board.

Clip the title to the end of a long spring and attach the spring to the bulletin board.

3-D Objects may be placed on shelves, in open boxes, or they may be caged or hung.

Bulletin Board People

Bulletin Board characters may have heads of equal size. Age many be indicated by the length of the body. For snappy characters, try using nonrealistic colors that are basic to the pattern of your bulletin board. Let your imagination be the guide.

Paper Sculpture Character

Construction paper

Coat hangers and paper circle or paper plate

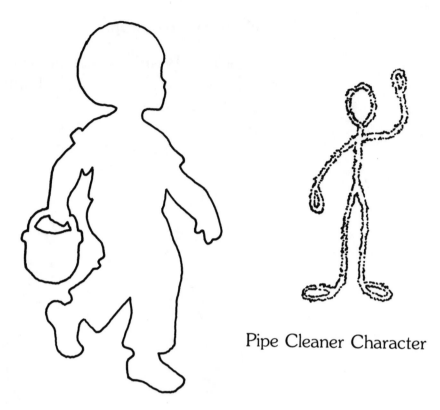

Pipe Cleaner Character

Silhouette Character

Faces can start with a circle, adding smaller circles, crescent shapes, straight lines, and paper fringe. With these elements every move becomes a new expression.

A face can look older by raising the eyes, a smile sour by reversing it, or a forehead worried by slanting its lines.

Kleenex Character

Wire Character

Stick figures can be made out of many varieties of materials.

Using boxes in different ways adds interest to bulletin board displays

"Pop outs" can be made by hinging the front of a box and inserting accordian-folded sheets

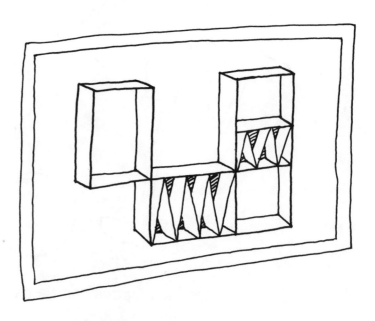

Attach the picture to the lid of a box.
Staple the box in desired position on
the board. Place the lid with the picture
attached, on the box.

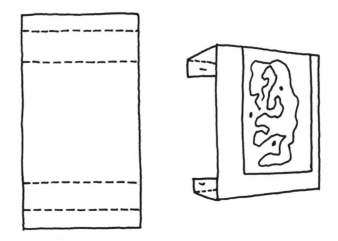

Use a piece of poster board, which can
be scored, bent curved, flexed, or
folded in a variety of ways. The picture
is attached to the poster board shape,
which is then stapled to the bulletin
board..

Cardboard folded, scored, and
stapled to the bulletin board

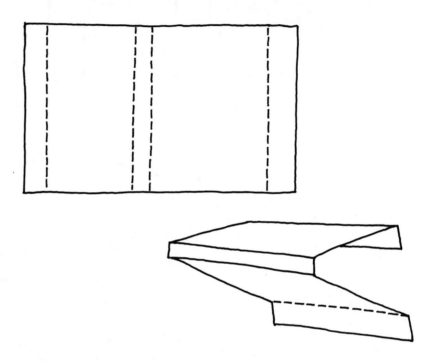

Folded and scored cardboard

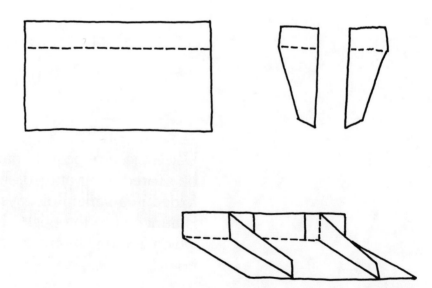

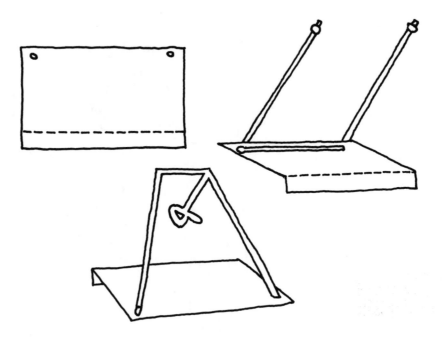

Yarn string, and wire are helpful
in making shelves

LETTERING

Lettering selected for titles and captions can
and should reflect the spirit of the bulletin board
display.

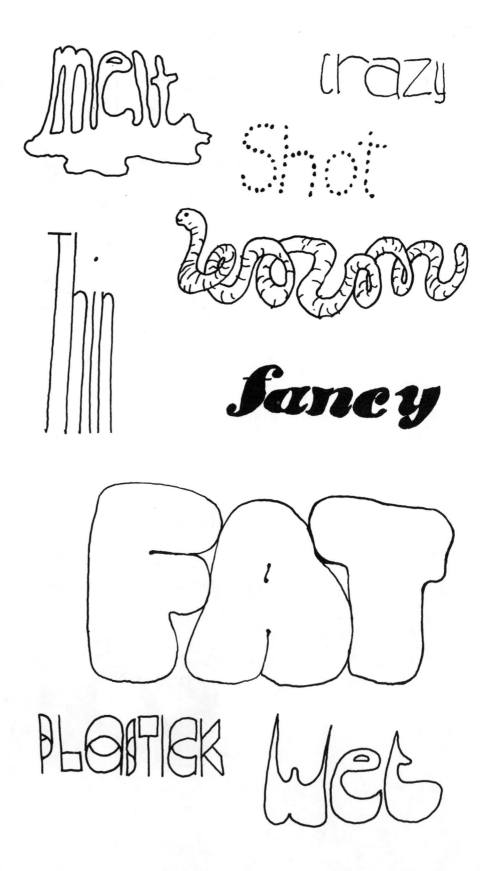

CUT LETTERS

To make these letters, fold paper and cut as pictured below.

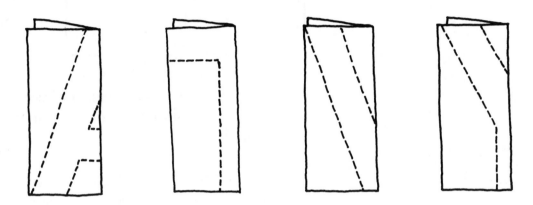

The letters "M" and "W" may be widened if desired.

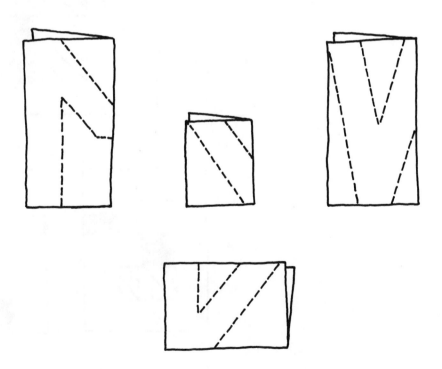

To cut a "two-window" figure, cut on fold as shown at left by cutting away the shaded area.

From this figure, the letters shown below may be made by unfolding and cutting away the solid shaded area.

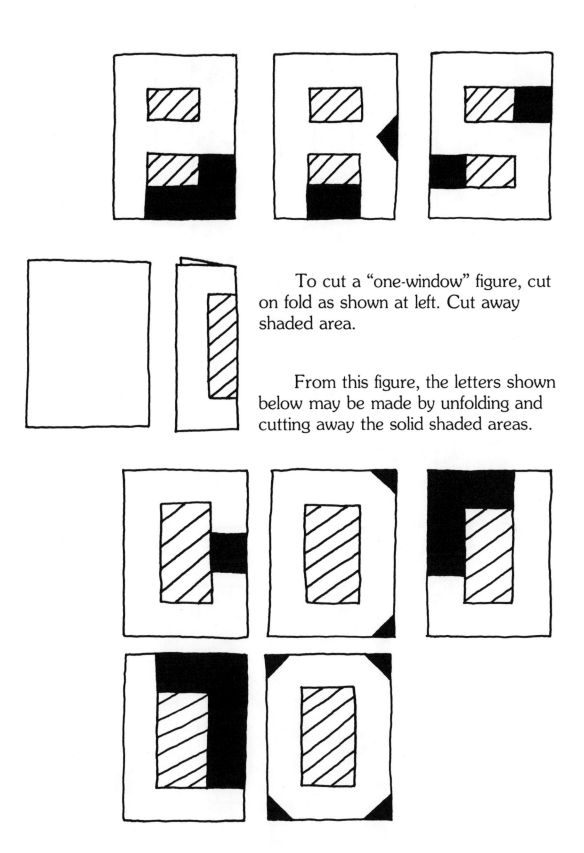

To cut a "one-window" figure, cut on fold as shown at left. Cut away shaded area.

From this figure, the letters shown below may be made by unfolding and cutting away the solid shaded areas.

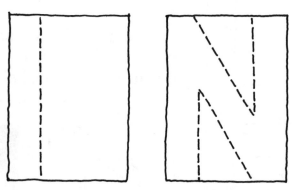

Do not fold paper to cut these letters.

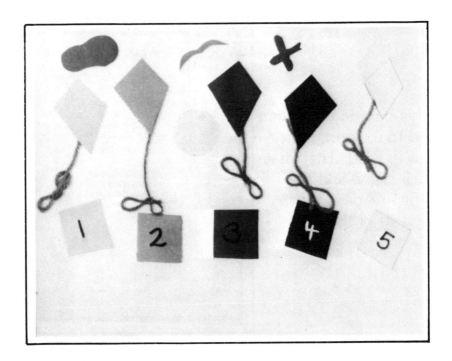

Five Little Kites

1,2,3,4,5
5 little kites up in the sky,
Said "Hi" to the clouds as they sailed by.
Said "Hi" to the birds as they sailed by.
Said "Hi" to the sun as they sailed by.
Said "Hi" to the airplanes as they sailed by.

Then whissh went the wind,
And they all took a dive,
1,2,3,4,5.

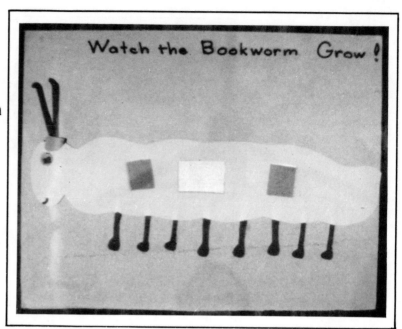

This bulletin board can be used to encourage children to read. They may sign their name and the book they read on the blank pages of the little book.

This bulletin board is one that is used to emphasize a classroom concept. This particular example can be used for first grade classroom to strengthen the use of the alphabet. Each student can create his/her individual examples to take home.

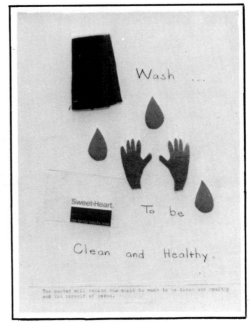

Holiday theme bulletin boards are used very often in elementary classrooms. Children can take part in the production of the bulletin board and can also make holiday gifts, cards, and projects dealing with the theme to take home.

CHAPTER 6
Puppetry

What is puppetry?

Puppetry is an art. Anything inaminated, when it is given life through the imagination, becomes a puppet. They are of many shapes, sizes and are operated in a variety of ways. The desire to make puppets is nothing new. People have been creating them for thousands of years. Why? People can express themselves through puppetry. It is also a means of communications, an extension of human expression.

When choosing the type of puppet with which you wish to work, you should first consider the nature and scope of each type of puppet, and the difficulties that may be met in construction and performance. You can make many different kinds of puppets from a variety of materials.

Some Common Type Puppets

1. Hand Puppets
2. Rod Puppets
3. String Puppets
4. Paper Mache Puppets
5. Paper Plate Puppets
6. Bag Puppets
7. Stick Puppets
8. Sock Puppets
9. Hand and Rod Puppets
10. Finger Puppets
11. Flat Puppets (Shadow Figure)

Paper plates can easily be turned into puppets with a little use of the imagination. Paper, yarn, felt, etc., can be pasted on the plate to create a puppet.

Papier maché puppets are relatively simple to make but require much more time, supervision, and space. Shreds of newspaper are soaked with wheat paste of a flour and water mixture and are then applied to the surface of an inflated balloon. Several layers are added to create a face. The heads are left to dry and when ready, they are painted and attached to bodies to make very nice puppets.

Some Basic Materials Needed for Puppetry may include:

1. Glue	5. String	9. Sticks
2. Paint	6. Bags	10. Socks
3. Yarn	7. Rods	11. Screws
4. Buttons	8. Crayons	12. Loops

13. Papier Maché Strips
14. Clay Forms
15. Cork
16. Wire
17. Nails
18. Cloth
19. Sewing Materials
20. Cardboard
21. Scissors
22. Anything else you want to decorate your puppet with can be used.

With the wide popularity of puppets as entertainers, those in the field of education should be aware of this medium and build upon its universal appeal. While entertainment value is important, there are greater values to be gained by making, using, and sharing puppets. Puppets make an excellent teacher, children listen to its pronouncements and admonitions more readily than to those of a human being. Through puppets, one becomes aware of the difficulty of communication between individuals. Puppets can also help an individual to be come aware of his own limitations. If a puppeteer creates a puppet who may be ugly and unpopular, perhaps he can identify with a fellow human who has this role in real life. While self-understanding is a consideration in the use of puppets, there are several concomitant learnings which aid an individual in his development. A child can develop certain manipulative skills and can achieve greater manual dexterity. Certain perceptive skills can be enhanced and the imagination can be further developed.

Thus puppets can serve as effective teachers. Teaching is not simply the outpouring of information, but the interrelationship of all who are involved in a teaching-learning situation so that ideas are understood and communicated.

As individuals speak through puppets, they reveal their understanding of the world in which they live, and thus give an indication of the concepts which they have assimilated. Thus puppets become more than activity, but rather serve to integrate many factors into the learning process. The educational values are continually being compounded as the individuals become involved in this stimulating activity.

PUPPETS

Objectives:

1. To introduce the child to the characters in their reading series.
2. To allow the child to expand his imagination by creating characters on their own.
3. To be able to create on their own what these characters mean to them.

Materials:

Popsicle sticks, paint, glue, scrap material, construction paper, scissors.

Procedure:

Cut circle for head and decorate the head in any manner. Then glue circle to the popsicle stick.

Materials:

Socks, glue, scrap construction paper, yarn, buttons, scissors.

Procedure:

Fit the sock over the child's hand and fold down his fingers. Mark with a pen the mouth, eyes, and nose should be. Then either paint or use construction paper to make the face.

Materials:

Brown paper lunch bag, newspaper, tape, glue, scrap material, yarn, buttons, construction paper, scissors, paper towel roll, tempera paint

Procedure:

Stuff the paper bag with newspaper, insert paper towel roll and tape.
Glue or paste on hair.
Finish up by painting or glueing on eyes, nose, mouth and clothes.

> NOTE: A long or big nose can be made by taking a small square of paper and wadding it into desired shape. Paint and glue on to the rest of the puppets.

Materials:

Paper plates, yarn, colored paper, glue or paste, buttons, feathers, and scissors.

NOTE: Any one or more of these may be used in making the puppet according to what you like.

Procedure:

Take a paper plate, decorate with eyes, nose, mouth, and hair. Strands of yarn can be used for the hair. Put a stick or paper towel roll on the back with either glue or staples. This makes a handy support for the puppet.

Other puppets can be made from: paper cups, Papier-maché heads, cloth bodies.

HAND PUPPETS

Objectives:

1. To provide each child with the opportunity of expressing new and different personalities through the character of a puppet.
2. To provide a culmination of the entire curriculum in producing a show through stage and scenery preparation, creative writing, expressive reading, muscular dexterity, artistic and musical ability used.

Materials:

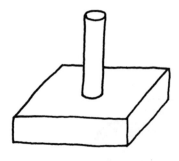

Clay
Stand to model clay on (A dowel stick or coke bottle may be used.)
Newspaper, funny paper, and paper towel strips, approximately ½" wide
Lubricant such as cooking oil, lard, shortening, vaseline, cold cream
Wallpaper paste
Tempera paint
Shellac
½ yard material
Small wire if desired for hands
Bottle corks (for wire hand wrists)
Masking tape

Procedure:

Papier-maché head and Neck

1. Model the clay into desired puppet head and

neck, exaggerating features.

2. Lubricate the wet clay with cooking oil.
3. Paste five layers of paper strips over the greased moist clay head alternating the different kinds of strips, ending with paper towel strips.
4. Allow to dry thoroughly.
5. Split the papier-maché head in half, cutting along the sides of the neck and head.
6. Shake out clay (in drying, the clay contracts when losing moisture and it should shake out easily.)
7. Join the halves together with additonal paper strips.
8. Allow to dry.
9. Paint with tempera.
10. Shellac for permanence.
11. Hair can be fashioned from yarn or curled paper strips.
12. Animal ears can be made from scrap leather.

Bodies

1. Make a simple sack-like construction from fabric with a drawstring at the neck to help attach to head.
2. The paws of animals may be included in the body form and stuffed to appear round.
3. The hands of "people" may be cloth mittens or wire frames covered with masking tape strips attached to a bottle cork at the wrist.
4. Paint and shellac covered wire hands.
5. Glue the cloth bodies to the papier-maché neck of the completed puppet head.

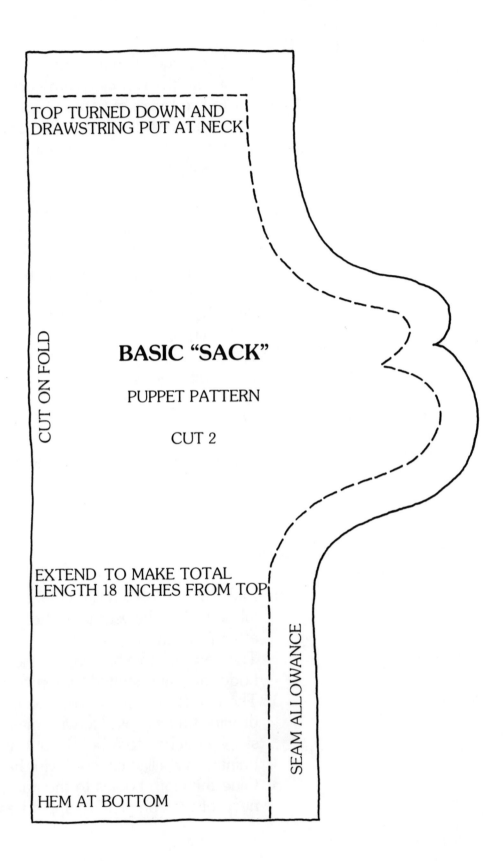

TOP TURNED DOWN AND
DRAWSTRING PUT AT NECK

CUT ON FOLD

BASIC "SACK"

PUPPET PATTERN

CUT 2

EXTEND TO MAKE TOTAL
LENGTH 18 INCHES FROM TOP

SEAM ALLOWANCE

HEM AT BOTTOM

Papier-Maché Puppet

(Refer to Cut and Paste
Chapter for specific papier-
maché directions)

Hand Puppets

Folded Paper Puppets

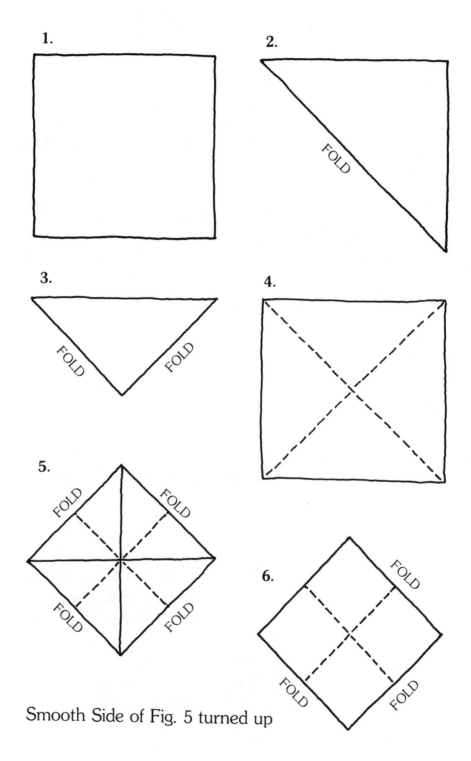

Smooth Side of Fig. 5 turned up

7.

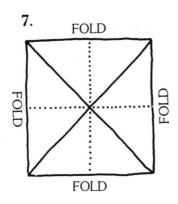

8.

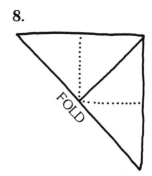

Fold Smooth Side Inside.

9.

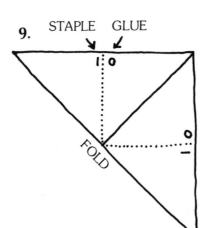

Drop Of Glue On Top
Sides Prevents Flapping.

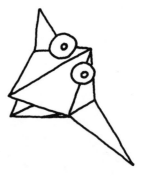

10.

Completed, Decorated Puppet.

NOTE: Line mouth if desired before stapling.
Pull out one inside corner for face front
after stapling.

CODE: ....Crease Line
CODE: .... 2 Cut Edges
CODE: O Drop of Glue
CODE: — Staple

Puppet Stages

CHAPTER 7
Clay

Clay is a material that will give many types of learning experiences. It offers the opportunity of experimenting and positive action in changing form to suit specific needs. It can be used over and over again so that the child becomes acquainted with it. Use will not destroy it and new and exciting possibilities appear each time it is used. It allows for experimenting with different tools; it can be used by one child or a group. It allows for self-expression and success. It stirs the imagination and its resistance is challenging. Working beside or with other children encourages communication and sociability. It extends concepts through experiences and learning of various types.

Clay is as revealing and exciting today as it was to primitive man. There is no real substitute for clay in an art program. It has a lasting influence on its creator. The manipulation of clay gratifies a basic need for children to work with their hands in the same sort of satisfying way they experience when playing in sand or making mud pies. Touching, pushing, and pulling the pieces of clay soon develops into an urge to make something.

The organization of materials is highly important due to the untidiness connected with clay work. Water base clay often has been ripened and worked to proper handling (clay tools, hairpins, popsicle sticks, skewer's, etc., can be used). Rags, pan of water, and plenty of newspaper for table should be readily available. Each child should be given a mass of clay—enough to handle easily in two hands. Each finished object should be thoroughly dry before firing.

Low-fire glazes are very successful in finishing the children's work. The dry glaze should be mixed with clean water to the consistency of whipping cream. Objects should be fired before applying glaze. Two or three coats of glaze should be applied to the fired objects, being careful not to glaze the underside unless stilts are used. The pieces are then fired a second time at the correct temperature in the directions for each particular glaze. Cones and/or a pyrometer are necessary for correct firing in the kiln.

Children should learn to handle clay in simple mass forms. Subject matter is secondary to simply, sturdy form. Simple instructions should be given. The clay should be kept in mass. Legs, arms, ears, and other appendages should be pulled out of the mass of clay in the forming figures. By pinching and pressing clay from the center of the mass, simple bowls can be formed. If it is necessary to work several days on an object, it can be wrapped in plastic or moist rag so that it stays moist until finished. The finished project should be simple. An old paint brush may be washed over the wet clay object for smoothing. Allow the clay to dry slowly.

If it is possible to have the clay fired and glazed, it is most desirable. If not, it may be painted with tempera or powder painting and then given three or four coats of shellac.

There are many different kinds of clays:

Clay — a natural earthlike material; the product of geological weathering surface of the earth.

Earthenware — a low-fired clay or a non-vitreous clay with an absorbency rate from 5-207.

Vitreous — state of non-absorbence.

Stoneware — high fired clay with little or no absorbency.

Porcelain — a very high-fired clay, totally vitreous with no impurities.

Bisque — once fired but unglazed clay.

Grog — crushed fired clay.

These are simple and basic techniques of pinching clay:

Pinch — squeezing clay with thumb and index finger.

Slab — rolling out flat strips of clay.

Coil — rolling thin lengths of clay with fingers.

Pressed — pressing sections of clay into pre-determined shapes.

Subtractive — using tools to take away from a solid mass of clay.

Additive — building a whole from small units of clay.

Modeling with clay seems to provide outlets for emotional tension. Its value as a manipulative material helps muscle development and the eye-hand coordination.

Working with clay is extremely valuable to the child. He can use the materials with his hands having to learn how to manage a tool such as a paintbrush. Clay also provides a sensory experience for a child. Examples: rolling, squeezing, pounding, and bending.

In the overall, the child will gain a new perspective.

Suggestions for a kindergarten class (suggestions for the teacher):

1. Use clay before giving it to your kindergarteners. Discover your feelings about using it and try to work through undesirable attitude. Find out the best consistency for clay. Learn how much water you need to add to make it feel just right.

2. Use the back of oilcloth or plastic on the table when working with clay. Give each child wishing to participate a ball of clay about the size of an orange. Too little is discouraging and too much is wasteful.

3. If working with moist clay, children usually make a ball and stick it to another ball to make a body and a head. When these "stuck together" parts dry, they usually fall

apart. You may need to help the child pull out clay to make a leg or a head. However, only a few children will be able to do it.

PAPIER-MACHÉ PULP

Newspaper
6 tbsp. flour or 6 tbsp. dry laundry starch
or 1 cup liquid starch
Knead till heavy dough consistency.
3-6 hrs. drying period

SAWDUST RECEIPE

15 heaping cups sawdust
15 heaping cups wheat paste
6 tbsp. salt
water
Put into huge container. Gradually add
boiling water, stirring constantly till
mixture looks like a stiff bread dough.
Makes: 30 balls

STARCH FINGER PAINT

1 lb. box gloss starch
1 cup soapflakes
1/2 cup talcum powder
4 qts. water
Mix together and cook till clear

SALT CERAMIC DOUGH

1 cup salt
1/2 cup cornstarch
3/4 cup cold water
Mix salt and cornstarch. Gradually add cold water. Do this in the top of a double boiler until consistency of bread dough achieved. Makes enough for 1 student. The material can be painted and can be easily rolled flat and cut out.

CLAY DOUGH

1 cup flour
1 cup salt
1 tbsp. alum
1 cup water
Powder or food coloring
Mix flour, salt, alum together. Add coloring and mix in water slowly. Makes small amount for one student.

Finished clay pieces are sources of satisfaction and achievement. Creative projects shared by a group develops a sense of appreciation for the contributions of others. Creative art experiences pull children upward to better and better accomplishments.

CHAPTER 8
Printing

Printmaking Activities

Printmaking is a process in which ink or paint is spread upon a prepared surface which in turn transfers an impression upon another surface by means of applied pressure.

Vocabulary

BRAYER — a rubber-covered roller used in inking metal plates, linoleum, and wood blocks.

COMPOSITION — the quality of being put together in such a way as to produce a harmonious, aesthetic whole.

LINOLEUM BLOCK — a piece of battleship linoleum into which an impression has been cut to be printed in relief.

MONOPRINT — a print obtained by making a single print from a plate upon which an impression has been created with paints, oils, or inks.

PLATE — a block, stone, stencil, or other material upon which an image has been carved, drawn or etched for the purpose of printing.

PROOF — a trial print obtained from a block, plate or screen for the purpose of being studied and corrected.

RELIEF PRINTING — a process of printing from a raised or projected surface.

FINGER PRINTING

Objective:

To allow children to use their imagination in creating pictures or designs with combined arrangements of finger prints.

Materials:

Paper, Ink pad or watercolor set, Pencil or India ink.

Procedure:

1. Dip fingers in paint or on stamp pad.
2. Press fingers on paper.
3. Finger prints may be combined to form design or they may be drawn into individual objects with the use of India ink and pen.

Finger printing allows children to use their imagination in creating pictures or designs with combined arrangements of finger prints. It allows the child to explore the many possibilities of arranging finger prints to form figures, objects, animals and people. Finger printing brings about an awareness of texture and demonstrates the fact that no two finger prints are exactly alike.

LEAF PRINTING

Objective:

To have children obtain an impression of the leaf on paper. Brings about awareness of texture.

Materials:

Leaves, Paint, Brayer, and Paper.

Procedure:

1. Spread paint evenly on surface of the leaf or leaves.
2. Lay painted leaf on paper (flat).
3. Cover leaf with white paper.
4. Roll over with brayer and print is complete.

LEAF PRINTING

Leaf printing is one means of increasing a child's awareness of the quality of texture. Leaf printing demonstrates how to create a balanced positive and negative image from natural forms. The idea of composition is also important in order that the child be able to create a pleasing arrangement of the leaf prints.

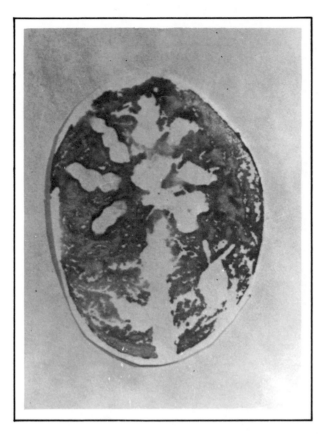

This method is achieved by cutting away part of the soft raw potato. Ink is put onto the surface. The child then presses the potato onto the paper creating a pleasing print.

POTATO AND LIME PRINTING

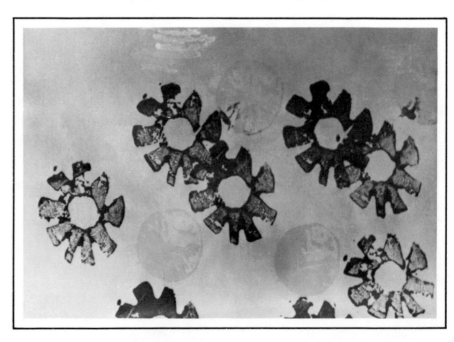

CARDBOARD PRINTING

Cardboard printing is an example of relief printing. Relief printing is a process of printing from a raised or projected surface, also a print obtained by such a process.

Objectives:

To explain the step by step process of relief printing to the children, and to let them use their imagination to obtain a pattern.

Materials:

1. Cardboard
2. Water base ink
3. Glue
4. Construction paper
5. Brayer
6. Exacto knife and Tray

Procedure:

1. Draw desired shapes on cardboard and cut them out.
2. Glue the shapes on a piece of cardboard
3. Roll the inked brayer over the shapes
4. Print design on paper.

CARDBOARD RELIEF PRINTING

This example of relief printing exposes the child to the step by step process of cutting a pattern of shapes from cardboard, gluing these shapes down on cardboard in an attractive arrangement, covering this pattern with paint and obtaining a print by pressing a piece of paper over the design. The child learns the quality of texture from the cardboard, and also the idea of composition in arranging his design.

LINOLEUM PRINTING

Objectives:

To teach children how to manipulate sharp tools in order to obtain a print from a linoleum block.

Materials needed:

Linoleum block, Linoleum cutting tools, Brayer, Water base printing ink and pen, Paper.

Procedure:

1. Draw design on the linoleum block (keep in mind that prints will come out backwards when printed).
2. Get out all parts you don't want printed. Whatever is not cut will appear on your print, anything cut away will not print.
3. Using the brayer, roll ink evenly onto the block.
4. Turn over and print on paper.

Linoleum printing is an example of relief printing. It teaches children how to manipulate sharp tools in order to obtain a print from a linoleum block. It lets the child use his imagination to design his own print. Linoleum printing demonstrates the use of a block to create a design which has a balance of positive and negative space.

CHAPTER 9
Textile Projects

Ideas:

Yarn and paste on paper
Collage with textile materials
Batik fabrics
Tie-Dye fabric
Yarn and material-sewing on paper (big stitches)
Yarn and material-pasting on paper

Adapt the above ideas for use in class:
For example use concepts such as: numbers,
colors, letters, animals, safety, names, families
and nature.

Collage with textile Materials

Yarn and Material on Paper

God's eye in the center—
yarn- wrapping around
popsicle sticks.

Color wheel using upholstery
samples

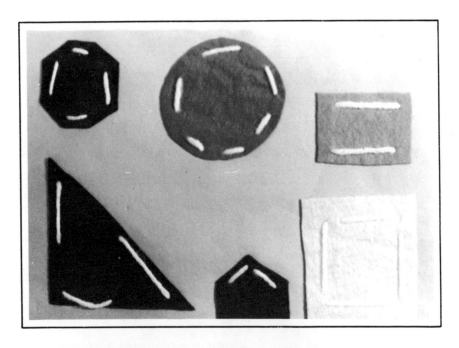

Yarn and material-sewing on paper. Big stitches develop fine
muscle coordination.

Ribbon weaving (instructions on next page)

Weaving with yarn on cardboard looms

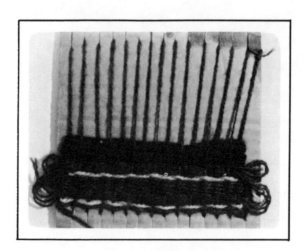

HAND-WOVEN RIBBON PILLOW DESIGNS

Materials Needed:

Muslin or some comparable cloth for a backing.
Ribbons of various widths and types. (i.e. satins, grosgrains)
Scissors, pins, a needle and thread
Outer Backing (i.e. Satin, Velvet)
Trims: lace, eyelet
Polyester

Steps to make a pillow

1. Decide on shape and size of pillow you are going to make and cut a piece of muslin to the appropriate size and proportion.

2. Experiment with ribbons by laying them out on the muslin. In this way you can decide which specific ones you want together and how you want the final design to look. Cut ribbons to the appropriate size and pin them on the muslin after having woven them over and under, under and over, alternating the pattern.

3. After pinning them to the muslin at the edges, stitch the design down, either by hand or machine, to make it permanent. Remove the pins.

4. Using an outer backing, pin it to your woven design, right sides together. Then sew it on all sides leaving an opening to turn your pillow and fill it with polyester fiber-fill.

5. After filling your pillow, stitch the opening closed by hand.

In addition to pillows, many gift items can be made using this weaving method. Examples of a few of these are: eye-glass cases, belts, shirt designs, key rings, etc.

TIE-DYEING

Materials:

Fabric, Rubberbands, Dye

Method:

1. Tie knots in fabric (secure these with rubberbands).
2. Dye fabric. Allow to stand 15 minutes.
3. Rinse fabric with cold water.
4. Remove rubberbands.
5. Allow fabric to dry and them iron.

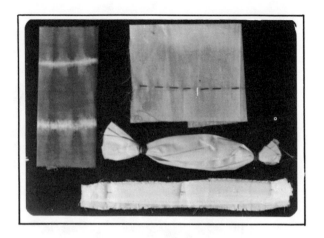

TIE-DYEING EXAMPLES

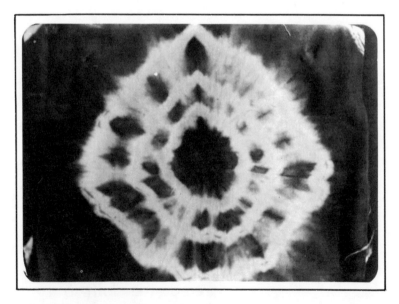

3 rubberbands

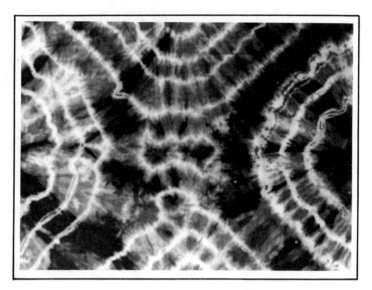

Corners folded to the center then rubberbands are wrapped.

BATIK

Materials:
Wax, Dye, Fabric, Brush, Newspaper, Iron

Method:

1. Lightly pencil-sketch your design on fabric.
2. Apply melted wax to design area. It is difficult to remove wax drips if they are in the wrong area on the cloth so try not to drip. Paint the small details in your design first.
   Remember, every area not covered by the wax will be dyed in the background color in the final result.

3. Let the wax on fabric semi-dry.
4. Run waxed design under cold water.
5. Put the wet, waxed fabric into the prepared dye-bath. Stir slowly for 5 minutes. Allow fabric to remain in dye for 15 minutes. (You may lengthen the dyeing time if darker shade is desired.) Remember the fabric will be 2 shades lighter when the batik process is finished.
6. Take fabric out of dye and rinse in cold running water until excess dye is removed.
7. Allow fabric to dry.
8. "Sandwich" the dried fabric between newspapers. Press *lightly* with a medium hot iron to remove wax.

1

3

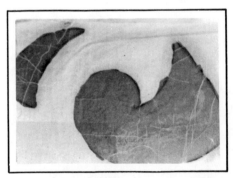

2

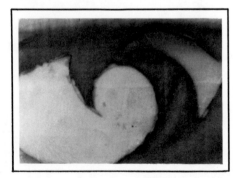

4

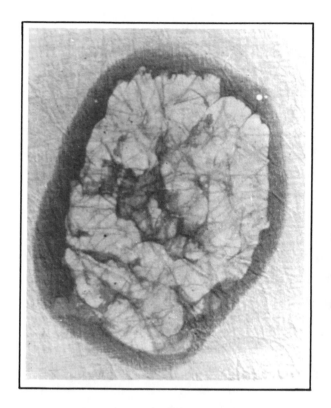 

WAX AND DRAWING BATIK

Materials:

Magic Markers, Wax, Dye, Fabric, Newspaper, Iron.

Method:

1. Draw with magic marker.
2. Cover entire design with melted wax.
3. Wet fabric with cold water.
4. Dye fabric. Allow to stand 15 minutes.
5. Rinse fabric with cold water.

6. Allow fabric to dry.
7. Place fabric between newspaper and iron to remove wax.

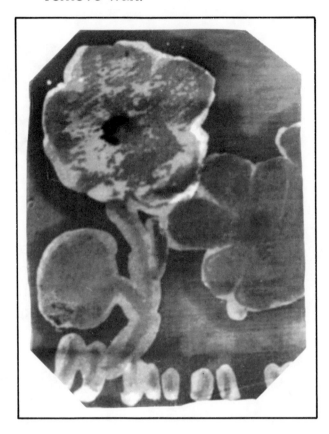

CHAPTER 10
Photography

The concept of photography is one which can amaze the human mind. A camera recalls more than any human eye can, therefore, children should be exposed to this "third eye."

Mock film that shows sequential motion
    Materials: paper (folded in accordion)
                 crayons
                 record
    Concept: camera stops action
    Artistic values: communicates feelings, actual experiences, line, color, rhythm
    Procedure: children dance to record; ask children to stop immediately when you stop music; draw stopped action on each fold of paper

Film making
    Materials: movie camera and film
    Concept: scriptwriting, producing, filming, splicing, developing

Artistic values: compositional qualities,
communicate feelings,
actual experiences
Procedure: plan and produce film

Mural slide projection
Materials: slides, large sheet of paper
crayons, leaves, sand, pebbles
Concept: enlargement
Artistic values: texture, realism, shapes
Procedure: project slides on paper on wall,
draw and color or paste objects
on paper to make mural

Field trips in classroom
Materials: slides from some event, art
museum, zoo, foreigh country,
national park
Concept: photographs as permanent record
of information
Artistic values: compositional quality,
viewpoint
Procedure: take children on trip via slide
show

Photograms
Materials: photographic paper, developer,
fixer, small found objects from
nature or class room
construction paper)
Concept: light sensitive paper, developing
process transparent and opaque
Artistic values: compositonal qualities,
unity, balance, contrast,
proportion, line

Procedure:

in dark room children arrange objects on paper, expose it to light and then develop it.

Design of opaque and transparent materials
    Materials: construction paper transparent plastic overhead projector
    Concept: transparent and opaque
    Artistic values: compositional qualities, balance, contract
    Procedure: demonstrate properties of opaque and transparent materials, students make a design using these and observe them on overhead projector

Flip book

        Materials: small pad of paper
                      crayons

        Concept: basics of film making, cartoons

        Artistic values: composition, repetitive
                      patterns

        Procedure: children decide on some action,
                      event, draw stages on successive
                      pages of pad, make only slight
                      changes in action each time, flip
                      through book to see action

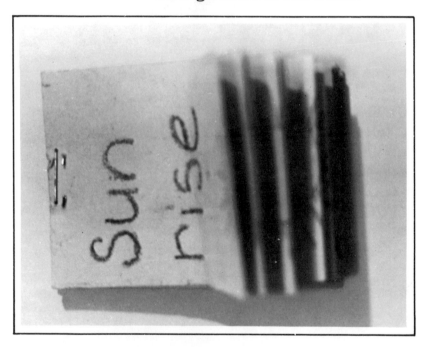

Slides from magazine photographs

        Materials: magazine photographs, clear
                      contact paper, hot water

        Concept: transparent and opaque

        Procedure: children lay clear plastic over
                      photograph and smooth com-

pletely to remove air bubbles,
soak in hot water about 5 minutes
and peel away paper, mount in
cardboard frame

Television
Materials: cardboard box, paper, crayons,
            paints, cardboard rolls from paper
            towels
Concept: principles of movie making,
            sequence splicing
Procedure: read story, take trip, establish any
            sequence of events, children draw
            one event, join together in
            sequence and roll through TV

Family tree from family photographs
    Materials: photographs, crayons, paper
    Concept: photograph as permanent record
          of reality self-concept
    Procedure: children bring in pictures of family,
          arrange to make family tree.

Slides to demonstrate color
    Materials: light cardboard, yellow, red and
                 blue cellophane, glue
    Concept: demonstrate primary and secondary
                 colors
    Artistic values: color
    Procedure: make a frame for squares of cello-
                 phane and use to overlap and
                 create new secondary colors.

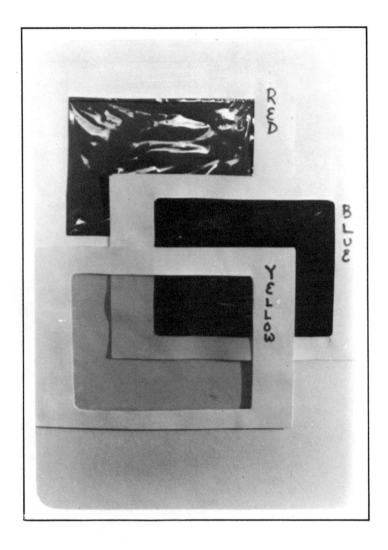

Field trips to take photographs
    Materials: instamatic cameras and film
    Concept: viewpoint, composing pictures,
          developing film
    Artistic values: compositional qualities, unity,
          balance, emphasis, space
    Procedure: discuss process of taking pictures,
          practice framing what you see
          with cardboard, discuss develop-
          ing and printing process, take trip.

Framing and mounting pictures helps the child learn to see the aesthetic quality of the work. He is proud of his work and framing and hanging the work adds to this sense of pride.

Collage of Magazine Pictures

Transparency

Color Lift

Ditto

References

The World Book Encyclopedia, Vol. 15-P Field Enterprises Educational Corporation, Chicago, 1967. pp. 797-799.

Nilsson, Harry. *The Point*. Dunbar Music, Inc., 1970.

Lowenfeld, Victor. *Creative and Mental Growth*. New York: The Macmillan Co., 1947.

About the Author

Dr. Jane A. Caballero is currently a professor in the Elementary Education Department at the University of Miami in Coral Gables, Florida. She has had extensive experience in providing art projects for young children. Art was an integral part of her curriculum in her primary classrooms in Hawaii, Texas, South Carolina, and Florida.

She received her M.Ed. from West Texas State University in Elementary Education with a minor in Art. She received her Ph.D. from the University of South Carolina in Early Childhood Education with a specialization in Art. She has received numerous art awards among which were the Tri-country Art Festival, first place; Sumter County Fair, first place; private showing and sales, Sumter Area Technical College; and Sumter Little Theater.

Dr. Caballero is a member of Kappa Pi National Art Fraternity, American Art Therapy Association, National Art Education Association, Florida Art Education Association, as well as early childhood professional organizations.

Dr. Caballero currently teaches Art for the Elementary School as well as other courses. She has presented art workshops in Orlando, Tallahassee, Jacksonville, and the Miami area. She is the art consultant for Camp Harmony and has provided art ideas for numerous other groups and associations, including the Miccosukee Indian Reservation and the Southern Association on Children Under Six.

She recently published *Extending Your Early Childhood Curriculum.*

About the Consultant/Photographer

Charles T. Caballero is an artist and teacher. He has has extensive training in art, receiving his B.S. in Art Education and his M.A. in Art, both from West Texas State University. He is currently working on a doctorate in Curriculum and Instruction specializing in Art and Media. He developed an art program in a high school in Texas, was art department head at Morris College, and has taught art to elementary, junior high, senior high, and college students in Florida. He has extensive experience in photography and has taught it on the junior college level.

He has received numerous art awards across the country, specializing in water color, enameling, and photography. He is a member of the Royal Society of Arts of Great Britain, Dade County Art Education Association, Enamel League South, in addition to many other professional organizations.

ORDER FORM

ORDER NO.	TITLE/DESCRIPTION	QUANTITY	PRICE

Subtotal . . . .

Ga. residents
add 4% sales tax . . . . .

Add shipping and
handling charges . . . . .

TOTAL . . . .

Make checks payable to:

HUMANICS LIMITED
P. O. Box 7447
Atlanta, Georgia 30309

Ship to:

NAME _____

ORGANIZATION _____

ADDRESS _____

CITY_____ STATE_____ ZIP_____

_____
(AREA CODE) TELEPHONE NO.

Institutional P.O. No._____

Date _____

Shipping and Handling Charges

Up to $10.00 add	$1.25
$10.01 to $20.00 add	$2.25
$20.01 to $40.00 add	$3.25
$40.01 to $70.00 add	$4.25
$70.01 to $100.00 add	$5.25
$100.01 to $125.00 add	$6.25
$125.01 to $150.00 add	$7.25
$150.01 to $175.00 add	$8.25
$175.01 to $200.00 add	$9.25

Orders over $200. vary depending
on method of shipment.

WE'LL HELP YOU TO HELP THEM.

EDUCATION

108-80 LOOKING AT CHILDREN. Richard Goldman, Ph.D.; Johanne Peck, Ph.D.; Stephen Lehane, Ed.D. Combines theory and practice, exploring such issues as language development, classification, play and moral development in children. Also includes a look at sex typing, television, single-parent families, and the fathers role in parenting. **$12.95**

407-80 ALTERNATIVE APPROACHES TO EDUCATING YOUNG CHILDREN. Martha Abbott, Ph.D.; Brenda Galina, Ph.D.; Robert Granger, Ph.D., Barry Klein, Ph.D. Delves into the theoretical basis behind three major programmatic approaches to education: programs emphasizing skill development; cognitive growth; and affective development. This book encourages the reader to develop his or her own theoretical and philosophical position. Each approach is discussed according to rationale and Philosophy, Curriculum Goals, Planning of Instruction, Use of Physical Space, Instructional Materials, Evaluation Methods, and the Instructional Role of the Teacher and Child. **$6.95**

413-80 YOUNG CHILDREN'S BEHAVIOR. Johanne Peck, Ph.D. Approaches to discipline and guidance to help the readers deal more effectively with young children. Six units focus on "Examining Your Goals," "Looking At Behavior," "Young Children's Views of Right, Wrong and Rules," "Applying Behavior Modification," and "Supporting Childs Needs." **$7.95**

406-80 THE WHOLE TEACHER. Kathy R. Thornburg, Ph.D. Designed for education majors and teachers of early childhood programs, this book presents a unified approach to teacher training. Topics addressed include: personal attitues, curriculum planning and development; classroom management techniques; working with volunteers, staff and parents; and professional development. **$12.95**

418-80 ORIENTATION TO PRE-SCHOOL ASSESSMENT. T. Thomas McMurrain. Designed for the child development center staff, this handbook presents a clear description of the effective assessment of the individual child. In addition, this manual is the user's guide to HUMANICS CHILD DEVELOPMENT ASSESSMENT FORM, a developmental checklist of skills and behavior that normally emerge during the 3 to 6 year range. Includes 5 assessment tools. **$14.95**

419A-80 COMPETENCIES: A SELF STUDY GUIDE FOR TEACHING COMPETENCIES IN EARLY CHILDHOOD. Mary E. Kasindorf. Divided into six competency areas and thirteen functional areas of competence as identified by the Child Development Consortium. This guide can be used to identify existing teaching skills and training needs. Designed to serve as an aid for those preparing for the C.D.A. credential. It contains checklists of teacher and child behaviors and activities that would indicate competence and can be used in assembling a C.D.A. portfolio. **$12.95**

humanics

Post Office Box 7447
Atlanta, Georgia 30309

PROJECT IDEAS

416-80 AEROSPACE PROJECTS FOR YOUNG CHILDREN. Jane Caballero, Ph.D. This "first of it's kind" manual provides teachers and young students with an overview of aerospace history from kites and balloons, on to helicopters, gliders and airplanes, through todays satellites and the space shuttle. Each chapter is followed by interdisciplinary activities and field trip suggestions. **$12.95**

403-80 MATH MAGIC. Filled with ideas for creating a stimulating pre-school learning environment, this book encourages active participation in the learning process. Through songs, limericks, puzzles, games, and personal involvement it will help children become accustomed to basic math principles, such as classification, seriation, the development of logical thinking, as well as teaching them basic problem solving skills. Comes with "Magic Pouch" which contains full size games, puzzles, bulletin board aids and whimsical animals (17 x 24) as a supplement to the text. **$12.95**

Vol. I, 409-80, Vol. II, 410-80. WHEN I GROW UP. Michele Kavanaugh, Ph.D. Provides activities for expanding the human potential of male and female students, while eliminating sex-role stereotypes. Volume I contains experiences for pre-kindergarten thru 8th grade students. Volume II continues with input suitable for high school through young adulthood.
$10.95 ea.

408-80 METRIC MAGIC. Kathy R. Thornburg, Ph.D. and James L. Thornburg, Ph.D. A fun book of creative classroom activities, *Metric Magic* was developed to teach preschoolers through sixth graders to think "metric." Includes action oriented activities involving the concept of length and progress through mass, area, volume, capacity, time, speed, and temperature. **$8.95**

417-80 ART PROJECTS FOR YOUNG CHILDREN. Jane Caballero, Ph.D. Over 100 stimulating projects for pre-school and elementary age children, including: drawing; painting; cut and paste; flannel and bulletin boards; puppets; clay; printing; textiles; and photography. Designed for those with limited budget and time schedule. Success oriented. $12.95

400-A CHILD'S PLAY. Barbara Trencher, M.S. A fun-filled activities and material book which goes from puppets and mobiles to poetry and songs, to creatively fill the pre-schoolers day. This handbook is a natural addition to a CDA or other competency-based learning program and has been used nation-wide for this purpose. $12.95

415-80 DESIGNING EDUCATIONAL MATERIALS FOR YOUNG CHILDREN. Jane Cabellero, Ph.D. A competency based approach providing over 125 illustrated activities encompassing language arts, health and safety, puppetry, math, and communication skills. Suggested functional areas and stated purpose for each activity make this a valuable tool for the CDA candidate. $14.95

PARENT INVOLVEMENT

419-80 FAMILY ENRICHMENT TRAINING. Gary Wilson and T. Thomas McMurrain. Designed for a workshop of six sessions, this program focuses on concerns for families today including communication, family relations, discipline, and developing self-esteem. Techniques such as role playing, small and large group interaction, and journals encourage participants to develop greater understanding of themselves and others. This package includes a manual for trainers, a participants "log" and the booklet "Dialog for Parents." $12.95

102-80 PARENTS AND TEACHERS. Gary B. Wilson. Offers strategies for staff trainers or anyone involved in parent or adult education. Included are training techniques which facilitate group interaction, team building, effective communication and self awareness. Designed to build a program promoting increased parent-staff interaction, each activity includes clear instructions, stated objectives, lists of materials and time requirements. $12.95

106-80 WORKING TOGETHER. Anthony J. Colleta, Ph.D. This practical handbook includes: plans for parent participation in the classroom; alternative approaches to teaching parenting skills; ideas for home based activities; and supplements to parent programs in the form of child development guides and checklists. $12.95

107-80 WORKING PARENTS. Susan Brown and Pat Kornhauser. Designed to make a positive impact on the family life of working parents, this book presents techniques which promote constructive and enjoyable parent-child interaction without disrupting the families daily routine. $12.95

24 Hour Direct Mail Service:
404•874•2176

420-80 BUILDING SUCCESSFUL PARENT-TEACHER PARTNERSHIPS. Kevin J. Swick, Ph.D., Carol F. Hobson, Ph.D. and R. Eleanor Duff, Ph.D. Deals with the issues of parent involvement by including: an in depth examination of the changing nature of parenting and teaching in recent decades — the emergence of the two-parent working family, the vanishing extended family, the one-parent working family, and a comprehensive plan for implementing successful parent-teacher programs. $10.00

ASSESSMENT

CD-507 CABS — CHILDREN ADAPTIVE SCALE. Bert O. Richmond and Richard H. Kicklighter. A testing tool for children ages 5-10 years. Created to measure skills in the following areas: (1) language development; (2) independent functioning; (3) family role performance; (4) economic-vocational activity and (5) socialization. Useful for enabling teachers to plan remediation for the child's level of adaptive behavior. Designed to be administered directly to the child.
Manual $19.95 Student Test Booklet $.65 ea.

ADOLESCENTS

411A-80 I LIVE HERE, TOO. Wanda Grey. Designed for the teacher who would like to improve the atmosphere in the classroom by helping each student to develop a more positive self concept. Themes such as "You Are One Of A Kind," "Know How You Feel," "You And Other People," "As Others See You," and "Using Your Creativity," will foster in children a better understanding of themselves and the people around them. $8.95

414S-80 H.E.L.P. FOR THE ADOLESCENT. Norma Banas, M.Ed. and J. H. Wills, M.S. Explores the underlying causes of the problems of the high school underachiever or potential dropout. Useful tests, programs and reading references are included to help identify "learning weaknesses" and promote "learning strengths." $6.95

humanics

Post Office Box 7447
Atlanta, Georgia 30309

SOCIAL SERVICES

302-80 ASSESSING STAFF DEVELOPMENT NEEDS. Gary B. Wilson, Gerald Pavloff and Larry Linkes. Provides a step-by-step methodology for determining the training needs of child development programs and planning their resolution. Tear-out worksheets and staff questionnaires will help clarify job descriptions and goal definitions, in conjunction with the needs assessment. $3.00

206-80 A SYSTEM FOR RECORD KEEPING. Gary B. Wilson, T. Thomas McMurrain and Barbara Trencher. Designed for family oriented social service agencies. This handbook is an integral part of HUMANICS Record Keeping System and should be used as a guide to proper use of the HUMANICS Record Keeping Forms. $12.95

201-80 INTERVENTION IN HUMAN CRISIS. T. Thomas McMurrain, Ph.D. Clearly presented intervention strategies based on an evaluation of crisis intensity and the response capacity of the individual or family. Rights, risks and responsibilities of the helper are also discussed. $6.95

MAINSTREAMING

404S-80 NEW APPROACHES TO SUCCESS IN THE CLASSROOM. Norma Banas, M.Ed. and J. A. Wills, M.S. A companion volume to Identifying Early Learning Gaps, designed for mainstream children in kindergarten through third grade. Includes activities structured to inspire the student who has experienced repeated failure and to help him or her acquire learning skills in the areas of reading, writing and arithmetic. Can be used in the classroom for the entire group or for a small group. $12.95

412S-80 LATON: THE PARENT BOOK. Mary Tom Riley, Ed.D. Presents a training plan for parents of handicapped children, designed to acquaint them with the resources, facilities, educational opportunities and diagnostic processes available to help them raise their children. This easy to read book will encourage parents to get involved. $12.95

New Publications

REALTALK: EXERCISES IN FRIENDSHIP AND HELPING SKILLS. George M. Gazda, Ed.D., William C. Childers, Ph.D., Richard P. Walters, Ph. D. A human relations training program for secondary school students including student text and instructor manual. REALTALK includes training in getting along with others, making and keeping friends, leadership, helping others deal with their problems, and learning how to talk with practically anyone about practically anything.

THE LOLLYPOP TEST: A DIAGNOSTIC SCREENING TEST OF SCHOOL READINESS. Alex L. Chew, Ed.D. A lollypop loved by all. Children will enjoy taking this test for school readiness, educators will appreciate the easy quick, and significant results. Purpose of the test: (1) to assist the schools in identifying children needing additional readiness activities before entering first grade (2) to identify children with special problems and (3) to assist schools in planning individual and group instructional objectives. Culture-Free.

SPECIAL INTRODUCTORY PRICE $14.95 each